M000084841

Arizona
WILDLIFE VIEWING GUIDE

Compiled and edited by
Sharen Adams
Sharon Mallman

Adventure Publications, Inc.
Cambridge, Minnesota

THIS BOOK IS DEDICATED TO DR. BRUCE D. TAUBERT

For 26 years Bruce Taubert has played a major role in the protection of wildlife and the remaining wild places in Arizona and across North America. This publication and countless other important projects related to wildlife conservation and outdoor recreation would not have been possible without his outstanding professional stewardship and dedicated service to the people of Arizona. The photos Bruce donated to this guide are a colorful reflection of his sensitive understanding and love for the great state of Arizona.

Heritage Fund

The Arizona Wildlife Viewing Guide was made possible through a grant from the Arizona Heritage Fund.

Book and cover design by Jonathan Norberg (all rights reserved)

Photo Credits: (all photos copyrighted by the respective photographers listed below, with all rights reserved)

Front cover photo: Gila Woodpecker by Cindy Marple

Back cover photos: American Pronghorn by Joe and Marisa Cerreta; American Buffalo, Desert Spiny Lizard and Acorn Woodpecker by Bruce D. Taubert; Bighorn Sheep by Ken Morgan

George Andrejko: 20, 21, 58-59 (Dead Horse Lake State Park) **Arizona State Parks:** 14 (bottom) **Randy Babb:** 16 (bottom) **Joe and Marisa Cerreta:** 24 **Michael Graybrook:** 231 (Apache Trout) **Susanna Henry/USFWS:** 96-97 (Kofa National Wildlife Refuge) **Don Jones:** 197 (Coues white-tailed deer) **Charles W. Melton:** 16 (top) **Bob Miles:** 28-29 (Vermilion Cliffs) **Chris Parrish:** 16 (middle), 57 (California condor) **William Radke:** 15 **Bruce Sitko:** 198-199 (Water Canyon Big Lake Loop) **Bruce D. Taubert:** 13, 14 (top), 17, 22, 123 (Gambel's quail), 124-125 (Saguaro National Park), 196 (Broad-tailed humming-bird) **Tom Whetten:** 23

All rights reserved, including the right to reproduce this book or any part thereof in any form, without the written permission of the publisher (except brief quotations for reviews).

10 9 8 7 6 5 4 3 2 1

Arizona Wildlife Viewing Guide
Copyright 2007 by Watchable Wildlife, Inc.
Published by Adventure Publications, Inc.
820 Cleveland St. S
Cambridge, MN 55008
1-800-678-7006
www.adventurepublications.net
Printed in China
ISBN-13: 978-1-59193-141-6
ISBN-10: 1-59193-141-X

ACKNOWLEDGEMENTS

The collection and compilation of the material contained in this book required the expertise, experience and hard work of a number of wildlife and administrative professionals. Watchable Wildlife Inc and the Arizona Game and Fish Department wish to thank the following individuals and their agencies for their help on this project.

Steering Committee

Bruce Taubert, Arizona Game and Fish Department, Chair

Sharen Adams, Arizona Game and Fish Department

Kerry Baldwin, Pima County Parks and Recreation Department

Ellen Bilbrey, Arizona State Parks

Bill Grossi, U.S. Bureau of Land Management

Bob Hernbrode, Arizona Game and Fish Commission

Amy Heuslin, U.S. Bureau of Indian Affairs

Melissa Maiefski, Arizona Department of Transportation

Jim Mallman, Watchable Wildlife, Inc.

William Radke, U.S. Fish and Wildlife Service

Special Thanks

In addition to the work of the Steering Committee a number of individuals donated expertise, services and photographic art that greatly enhanced the look and content of this publication. We want to especially thank the following for their contributions to this viewing guide: William Radke, Julie Hammond, Troy Corman, Randy Babb, Bruce Sitko, Mark Zornes, Mike Rabe and Tom Brennan.

GOVERNOR'S LETTER

January 2007

Dear Readers,

As Governor of this beautiful state, I extend an invitation to all of you to spend some time in Arizona's great outdoors and enjoy our remarkable wildlife resources and scenery. From the majestic Grand Canyon to the peaks of the White Mountains and remote stretches of the Sonoran Desert, Arizona boasts an incredible variety of wildlife species, many found nowhere else in the United States. Watching wildlife is one of the fastest growing outdoor activities and has become an economic boom to many rural communities. From bird watchers to campers and hikers, all outdoor recreationists enjoy seeing wild animals in wild places.

With a little help, wildlife can become significantly more visible to us. Let the color photos, maps and wildlife-viewing tips in this book guide you in your journey to find many of Arizona's wild areas and animals.

The *Arizona Wildlife Viewing Guide* will help you find:

- the California condor with its nearly 10-foot wingspan in the canyon areas of northern Arizona
- the incredibly beautiful elegant trogon in the Huachuca Mountains
- winter sunrise flights of sandhill cranes over Wilcox Playa and Whitewater Draw
- majestic desert bighorn sheep along the shores of Lake Mead and Lake Havasu
- the unique birds in our southeastern Arizona sky islands
- bugling elk in high elevation mountain meadows
- and much, much more.

So grab your binoculars, camera, a field guide or two and get out there; there is wildlife to be seen, enjoyed and appreciated.

Yours very truly,

Janet Napolitano
Governor

4

"TO HELP COMMUNITIES AND WILDLIFE PROSPER"

A simple mission statement for a complex challenge; Watchable Wildlife Inc. is an independent nonprofit working with communities and state and federal wildlife agencies across North America. We help these agencies and organizations better utilize their wildlife and wild places.

We accomplish this mission by developing sustainable wildlife viewing programs with our partners. Our areas of focus are our annual conference, publications and on-the-ground projects.

Our annual Watchable Wildlife Conference is the nation's best vehicle for presenting new ideas. It also serves as an international forum for training and recognizing the works of professionals in the field of wildlife viewing. Watchable Wildlife Inc. works hands-on with conservation-minded partners on projects across the continent to develop safe, satisfying and sustainable wildlife viewing.

Our Viewing Guide Series is a continent-wide effort to meet the needs of North America's growing wildlife viewing public. The guides encourage people to observe wildlife in natural settings and provides them with information on where to go, when to go, and what to expect when they get there. We believe the presence of wildlife viewing sites near communities has positive social and economic impacts.

We want wildlife viewing to be fun. However, we also believe it should be an economically viable resource for the host community. In the larger context, we want people to learn about wildlife, to care about it and to conserve it.

For more information about Watchable Wildlife Inc., this year's conference, our other publications and our current projects, visit www.watchablewildlife.org.

Yours truly,

James Mallman
President, Watchable Wildlife, Inc.
www.watchablewildlife.org

Brown road signs with the binoculars logo let travelers know that they're in a great spot to see some wildlife! These uniform signs are officially approved by the National Department of Transportation and are one example of the programs sponsored by Watchable Wildlife, Inc.

Table of Contents

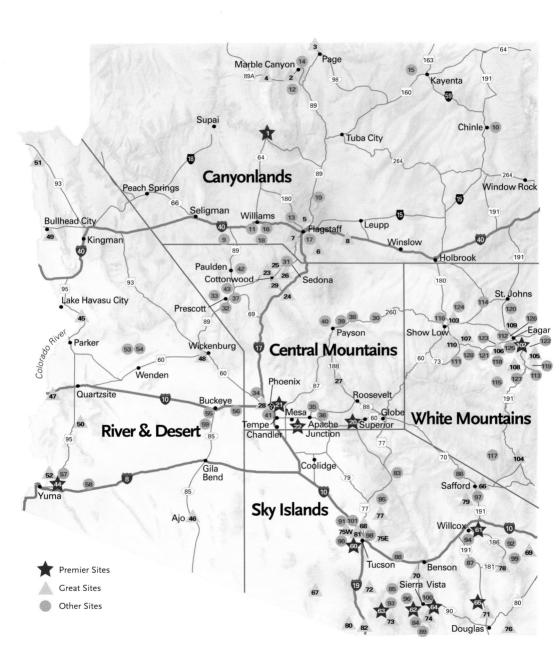

Marble Canyon 14 · Page 3
89A 4 · 2 · 15 · 163
12 · 98 · Kayenta · 191
160 · 59
89

Supai · Chinle 10
1 · Tuba City
18 · 64 · 264 · Window Rock
51 · 89 · 264
93 · Canyonlands · 191

Peach Springs · 180 · 19 · 15
66 · Seligman · Williams 13 · 5 · Leupp · 191
Bullhead City · 40 · 11 · 16 · Flagstaff
49 · Kingman · 9 · 18 · 7 · 17 · 8 · Winslow · 40
40 · 89 · 6 · Holbrook · 191
Paulden · 42 · 25 · 31
95 · 93 · Cottonwood · 23 · 26 · Sedona · 180
Lake Havasu City · 33 · 43 · 37 · 29 · 24 · 124 · St. Johns
45 · Prescott · 32 · 69 · 116 · 103 · 114 · 120 · 126
89 · 40 · 39 · 38 · 30 · 260 · 109 · Eagar
Parker · Wickenburg · 17 · Payson · Show Low · 107 · 123 · 112 · 122
53 · 54 · 48 · Central Mountains · 110 · 106 · 125 · 102 · 105
60 · 188 · 60 · 73 · 111 · 128 · 121 · 118 · 108 · 119
Wenden · 60 · 27 · 115 · 127 · 113
Quartzsite · Phoenix · 87 · Roosevelt · 191
47 · 34 · 88 · Globe · White Mountains
50 · Buckeye · 28 · 41 · Mesa · 35 · 60 · 117 · 104
95 · 55 · 56 · 36 · Apache · 20 · Superior
59 · Tempe · 22 · Junction · 77 · 70
River & Desert · 85 · Chandler · Coolidge · 79 · 83 · 86 · Safford · 66
52 · 57 · Gila · 10 · 95 · 97
44 · 58 · Bend · Sky Islands · 77 · 79
Yuma · 85 · 77 · Willcox · 10
Ajo 46 · 91 · 101 · 68 · 94 · 61 · 186 · 92
75W · 81 · 98 · 75E · 191 · 99 · 69
90 · 60 · 88 · Benson · 87 · 181 · 78
Tucson · 70
67 · 19 · 72 · 85 · Sierra Vista · 80
93 · 96 · 100 · 64 · 65 · 71
63 · 62 · 74 · 90
80 · 82 · 73 · 84 · 89 · Douglas · 76

★ Premier Sites
▲ Great Sites
● Other Sites

Colorado River

6

Table of Contents

Number indication on map: ★ Premier Sites   ▲ Great Sites   ● Other Sites   **7**

Number indication on map: Premier Sites Great Sites ● Other Sites

Bill Williams National Wildlife Refuge

PHOTO BY WILLIAM RADKE

Spectacular Arizona

Where are you?

As you look into the spotting scope, the jewel-like colors of a magnificent humming-bird capture your eye. Are you exploring a Mexican forest? No.

The whistling bugle of a rutting bull elk has just shattered the icy morning silence. Are you camping in the Canadian Rockies? No again.

The antics of a cactus wren have entertained you all morning. Are you hiking in the Utah desert? Closer, but no.

Your heart thrills to the whispered song of wind in the feathers of a soaring California condor. Where in the world are you? In Arizona, where the wildlife watching is as grand as the sunsets are beautiful.

Arizona wildlife watchers know the Grand Canyon State is a special place to watch wildlife. No need to travel all the way to Canada to hear elk bugling in autumn, when you can explore the White Mountains of eastern Arizona instead. Why go to Mexico to view rare hummingbirds, when the same birds grace the mountains of southern Arizona? And here, where the four American deserts meet, you can make your acquaintance with all sorts of scaly, slithering and singular creatures. Bowled over by bats? Arizona boasts 28 species, one fewer than Texas. Fascinated by snakes? We have 52 species, from "A" (Arizona black rattlesnake) to "Y" (Yaqui black-headed snake).

Wildlife watching in Arizona takes place in wild scenery. A herd of javelina passes beneath a flowering saguaro silhouetted against a saffron-colored sunset. A shy desert bighorn sheep drinks from the Colorado River beneath sheer canyon cliffs. A white-tailed deer peers around a towering ponderosa pine.

Dust lifts under the hooves of a herd of pronghorn sprinting across a wide-open grassland. The golden eyes of a mountain lion burn like flames as the big cat paces between red canyon rocks. From shifting sand deserts to treeless mountaintops, from the Grand Canyon to the San Francisco Peaks, to the Sky Islands of southern Arizona … Arizona is a gorgeous place to watch wildlife.

Desert Crossroads

When most people think of Arizona, they picture the bare cliffs of the Grand Canyon, the strange shapes of saguaro cactus or the distinctive diamond pattern on the back of a rattlesnake. In other words, the picture of Arizona that we carry in our minds was taken in a desert.

Arizona boasts many forested areas, including the largest contiguous stand of ponderosa pine in the world, but people are right to imagine a desert when they think of the Grand Canyon State. In fact, North America has four deserts—the Sonoran, Mojave, Chihuahuan and Great Basin—and they all meet here.

Saguaro Cactus

Sonoran Desert (central Arizona) This is the most biologically diverse of the four deserts and the one most closely identified with classic American desert scenery. Its prominent feature is the saguaro cactus, the largest columnar cactus in the United States. A really large saguaro might stretch 80 feet skyward from its shallow, wide root system. Mesquite, paloverde and ironwood trees are other typical plants found here. They thrive in this, the hottest and wettest of the four deserts, with its two rainy seasons (in summer and winter) breaking up the desert drought.

Great Basin Desert (northern Arizona) The cold-est of the four deserts, the Great Basin reaches down from Colorado into northwestern Arizona in a series of basins and mountains. Most precipitation in this cold, arid desert is in the form of snow. This is sagebrush rather than cactus country, and its frigid, dry conditions do not encourage diversity among either plant or animal species.

Chihuahuan Desert (southeastern Arizona) The largest North American desert at more than 200,000 square miles, the Chihuahuan Desert extends up from Mexico into Texas, New Mexico and southeastern Arizona. A little higher in elevation than the Sonoran desert, it typically receives rain mainly in summer. Plants and animals here have to be both cold- and drought-resistant. You won't see a columnar cactus like the saguaro here, but you will see many small cacti, including yucca- and agave-type plants.

Mojave Desert (western Arizona) The dominant desert in California and Nevada, the Mojave is the smallest of the four North American deserts, totaling just 25,000 square miles. Like the Great Basin Desert, it is colder and dryer than the Sonoran Desert. Hardy plants like creosote and Joshua tree can get by on the small amount of rain, which falls predominantly in winter.

Elf Owl

Typical birds you might see in Arizona deserts include Harris's and red-tailed hawks, Gambel's quails, turkey vultures, Costa's hummingbirds, gilded flickers and Gila woodpeckers. Arizona deserts are also home to cactus, canyon and rock wrens; crissal and curve-billed thrashers; and western screech- and elf owls.

Hardy animals found throughout Arizona deserts include desert bighorn sheep, coyotes, mountain lions, bobcats and gray foxes. Ringtails, raccoons, badgers, black-tailed jackrabbits and desert cottontails also live in Arizona deserts, along with white-throated wood rats, Botta's pocket gophers and several species of skunks, mice, kangaroo rats and squirrels.

Snakes and lizards are probably the wildlife most often associated with deserts. They are most active during the warm part of the year (generally March through October.) The Gila monster, the only poisonous lizard found in the United States, is fairly common but tough to spot because it spends most of its time underground. Rattlesnakes are more common, more visible, and (especially as summer begins) more active. Lizards are easy to see and safer to approach; the best season for viewing them is spring, as temperatures warm. The large, slow chuckwalla and the small, quick common side-blotched and zebra-tailed lizards are three of many species found in Arizona deserts.

Watching wildlife in desert country

In a parched landscape, how does wildlife survive? Some animals have adapted to the dry conditions by reducing their water needs. For example, kangaroo rats produce water from the dry seeds they eat and can survive their entire lives without ever drinking free-standing water. These amazing rodents also reduce their water need by living nocturnally (being active at night) and not venturing aboveground in the heat of day, common strategies also used by other small mammals.

Animals also adapt to the dry conditions by slowing their metabolism (going into torpor) to reduce the need for food and water, concentrating their urine to reduce the amount of liquid lost, and getting water from strange places (javelina satisfy their thirst with the soft pads and sweet fruit of prickly pear cactus.)

Riparian

Most animals do need water, though. And even in a desert, water can be found in lakes or ponds and in seasonal and year-round rivers. Rivers are especially important to animals and to resident and migratory birds. Over 80% of all birds use riparian habitat. In Arizona, only 1% of the land area is riparian, but these narrow strips of habitat along streams sustain more

Dead Horse State Park

plants and animals than any other habitat type. Some are free-flowing rivers fed by runoff or springs. Others are usually dry, drawing extra moisture provided by runoff from seasonal rains. Even these "dry riparian" areas support more plants than adjacent areas do, providing a haven for wildlife.

Mountains

Another strategy used by desert-dwelling birds and animals in the heat of summer is to move into the mountains. Go up several thousand feet in the space of a few miles and you're in a different world, one that is cooler and more moist. In southern Arizona, every 1,000 feet of vertical elevation gained means rainfall increases at a rate of about 4 or 5 inches, and temperature drops at a rate of 3 to 4 degrees. A 100° day in Tucson is a bearable 75° on nearby mountaintops. This elevational break in heat and the added moisture are crucial to some species, which survive on mountain ranges surrounded by seas of desert and grassland. The phenomenon of mountain ranges as islands gives rise to the term "sky islands," now popularly used to describe such ranges in the deserts of southern Arizona and northern Mexico.

Santa Catalina Mountains

Don't forget the forests

Though the picture in most of our minds when we think of Arizona is often a picture of the desert, the northern half of the state is graced by forests. And not just one kind of forest, either: Arizona is home to majestic, tall ponderosa pine forests, whispering forests of mixed conifers, sun-splashed oak woodlands, and wide-open areas of juniper and pinyon pine.

These forests are great for wildlife watching. Rocky Mountain elk and mule deer are found among the trees, as are javelina, many kinds of squirrels, waterfowl and songbirds. When you think of watching wildlife in Arizona ... don't forget the forests.

What does all this mean for wildlife watching in Arizona? Three things: first, because many animals are nocturnal, don't waste time looking for wildlife in the heat of day, especially during the summer. Instead, be active when animals are, looking for wildlife around sunrise and sunset when the air is cooler. Second, because most wildlife needs water, seek them along riverbeds and by lakes, ponds, or other water features. And finally, when it's hot in the desert, climb into the mountains. These strategies will improve your odds of seeing wildlife—and keep you more comfortable in Arizona's hot, dry climate as well.

Wildlife Worth Celebrating

From tiny, jewel-like hummingbirds to immense California condors with 9½-foot wingspans, and from white-throated wood rats to fleet-footed pronghorns to secretive mountain lions, Arizona has many kinds of wildlife worth celebrating. Here are just a few that you might encounter when watching wildlife in the Grand Canyon State.

Costa's Hummingbird

Hummingbirds

The bright turquoise-green gorget and violet-purple crown of a rare magnificent hummingbird flashing in the sunlight is a sight to remember. Arizona is host to 18 species of hummingbirds—more than any other state except Texas. The mountains of southern Arizona are widely known as great places to see hummingbirds, particularly in the spring and summer. Bring spotting scopes or binoculars to get up close and personal with these flying jewels.

California Condor

California Condors

It is difficult to appreciate how large the California condor is until you see one, but once you do, it is impossible not to be impressed by this king of the skies. Once so close to extinction that the few remaining birds were taken into captivity for a last-ditch captive breeding program, the condor now flies again in Arizona (as well as other western states and Baja California). Look for them spring through fall at the South Rim of the Grand Canyon, soaring or perched on a rock between the El Tovar Hotel and Lookout Studio. Year-round, but especially in winter, condors may also be seen at the Vermilion Cliffs release site viewing area, three miles north of U.S. Highway 89A on BLM Road 1065.

Desert Iguana

Amphibians and Reptiles

Arizona has a remarkable assortment of amphibians and reptiles, with 25 native species of amphibians and 107 native reptiles.

More than one third of the world's rattlesnakes (13 species) are native to Arizona. These highly venomous snakes include the sidewinder and the elegant and colorful Arizona ridge-nosed rattlesnake (the state reptile.) But most snakes in the state are harmless to humans, including several tiny "sand swimmers," aquatic gartersnakes and snake-eating kingsnakes.

Forty-nine species of lizards are native to Arizona, the most famous being the Gila monster. The visitor's chances of seeing one are small, as the Gila monster spends most of its time underground where it's cooler. Other well-known lizards include the desert iguana and chuckwalla, both residents of the state's hotter, lower desert areas.

The desert tortoise, ornate box turtle, painted turtle and three species of semi-aquatic mud turtles live in Arizona. The state is also home to 24 types of native frogs and toads, a remarkable number in a state better known for its dry environment. For tips on viewing amphibians and reptiles, see "Viewing Tips."

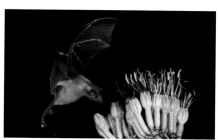

Long-nosed Bat

Bats

You may never see a bat while watching wildlife in Arizona, but you might hear them. Some bats use echolocation tones that are audible to humans. If you do see bats, it's most likely at dusk, when a cloud of these flying mammals comes pouring from the entrance of a cave or other structure where a colony is roosting. Whether you see or hear bats or not, you'll be glad they're here. Some bats are important pollinators, while others scoop insects from the sky (a bat can consume from ¼ to ½ of its body weight in insects each night.) Twenty-eight species of bats are found in Arizona at some time of the year. Bats can be found all across our state in every type of Arizona habitat, from deserts to forests. Arizona was the first state to have a full-time position within its state wildlife agency specifically designated to work with bats.

Places to Go

Arizona is home to many kinds of wildlife, from the denizens of its four deserts to the forest-dwelling animals found on its sky islands and in its northern mountains. The many places described in this book comprise the best of the best, a sampling of all Arizona offers to the wildlife watcher. In this book, the reader will find:

National Parks, Monuments and Recreation Areas

The U.S. National Park Service, within the Department of the Interior, manages two national parks and many national monuments and recreation areas in Arizona. The most well-known national park is the Grand Canyon, home to the California condor. Other areas noted for their wildlife-watching opportunities include Chiracahua National Monument in southwestern Arizona and Lake Mead National Recreation Area in northwestern Arizona.

Wildlife Refuges

The U.S. Fish and Wildlife Service, also within the Department of the Interior, manages eight national wildlife refuges in Arizona. Most are on the western edge of the state, along the Colorado River. Here you will find water-loving birds such as kingfishers, cormorants, egrets, herons and rails.

National Forests

The U.S. Forest Service, within the Department of Agriculture, manages six national forests in Arizona. These are the Apache-Sitgreaves, Coconino, Coronado, Kaibab, Prescott and Tonto. The term "national forest" can be somewhat misleading when applied to Arizona forests: in parts of the Tonto National Forest, for example, the traveler sees more cacti than trees. National forests make fine wildlife watching areas and often provide campgrounds and other amenities.

State Parks

The Arizona State Parks manages parks and natural areas statewide. Patagonia Lake State Park in southern Arizona is one of the best-known birding areas in the state, with giant Fremont cottonwood, willow, velvet ash and Arizona walnut trees sheltering many kinds of warblers, along with vermilion flycatchers, great blue herons and other birds. Catalina State Park provides wildlife opportunities of a drier kind: its mature mesquite bosque surrounded by saguaro and paloverde is home to mule deer, red-tailed hawks, Gambel's quail, cactus wrens and Gila woodpeckers.

Southeastern Arizona Birding Trail

Created by a partnership between land management agencies and bird conservation organizations, the Southeastern Arizona Birding Trail guides visitors through a diverse, spectacular region of southeastern Arizona. The map and descriptions lead visitors to 52 sites, offering information about habitat types, visitor amenities and suggestions for the best seasons to visit each site. It is available for $3 from the Tucson Audubon Society, the Southeastern Arizona Bird Observatory and other sources.

Wildlife Areas

The Arizona Game and Fish Commission owns or manages more than 260,000 acres of land. This entails 34 wildlife areas scattered all around the state. Most wildlife areas are available for public use, including wildlife viewing. These range from Sipe White Mountain Wildlife Area in the forests of northeastern Arizona, where elk, mule deer and turkey roam, to White Water Draw Wildlife Area in the grasslands of south-central Arizona, where white-tailed deer, black-tailed jackrabbit and bobcat are found. Wildlife areas are accessible free of charge, but visitors should be aware that there is little available in the way of restrooms, interpretive signage, or other developed facilities. The aforementioned Sipe White Mountain Wildlife Area near Springerville and White Water Draw Wildlife Area near Elfrida are two exceptions. Sipe has extensive foot trails and a visitor center, while White Water Draw has spotting scopes and viewing decks from which visitors can enjoy the numerous waterfowl that frequent the area. Specific questions regarding wildlife areas should be directed to regional Game and Fish offices. Wherever you are traveling, there is likely a Game and Fish Department wildlife area nearby.

Important Bird Areas

The National Audubon Society, in partnership with BirdLife International, is identifying a network of sites in the United States that provide critical habitat for birds. This global effort known as the Important Bird Areas Program (IBA) has been initiated in all 50 states. More than 1,900 state-level IBAs encompassing more than 140 million acres have been identified, with a goal of 3,000 designated IBAs. The IBA Program sets science-based priorities for habitat conservation and promotes positive action to safeguard vital bird habitats. The Arizona IBA Program is run by Tucson Audubon Society in coordination with the Audubon Arizona State Office and the IBA program.

The IBA Program identifies the most important sites for implementation of large-scale conservation efforts to ensure the protection of bird species in all habitats. Important Bird Areas provide essential habitat for one or more bird species and include sites for breeding, wintering and/or migrating birds. IBAs may be a few acres or thousands of acres in size, but usually they are discrete sites that stand out from the surrounding landscape. IBAs may include public or private lands or both, and they may be protected or unprotected.

If a site in this book is within an IBA, it will be noted in the site description with the above logo.

Since nearly all wildlife watching is done outdoors, there are a few guidelines that will add greatly to the comfort and enjoyment of your watchable wildlife experience. Arizona is a state of extremes and can be an inhospitable place for the unprepared. Here are a few suggestions to help make your visit a success.

Temperatures

Much of Arizona is desert—and warm season temperatures can become very uncomfortable, in excess of 120° during June and July in the southwestern part of the state. Most people and wildlife are smart enough not to be out on those days. But even a day that starts out mild may end hot—it is not unusual for early spring and late fall temperatures to reach into the 80s or 90s.

Proper clothing will help keep you cooler and more comfortable. As a rule, if the temperatures are below body temperature (98.6°), less clothing (shorts and T-shirts) will keep you cooler. When air temperature is higher than body temperature, long pants and sleeves are a better choice. A long-sleeved cotton shirt with a collar is far more versatile than a T-shirt. The collar can be turned up and sleeves rolled down for additional protection from the sun. There are even shirts that provide protection from the sun and have an SPF rating.

Sunscreen is useful when spending time outdoors, regardless of the cloud conditions or temperature. Be sure to replace the lotion as it is sweated or worn off. Since it is nearly always sunny in Arizona, most people find wide-brimmed hats indispensable. Loosely woven straw types with ventilation holes near the top will keep your head cooler.

It's smart to plan for the heat, but in Arizona one must prepare for the cold as well. Though daytime temperatures are generally pleasant on most winter days, it can get surprisingly chilly at night and during the early morning hours. This often catches visitors unprepared, so plan ahead and bring along layers.

Mormon Lake

Conversely, Arizona has much in the way of higher elevations, and like mountainous regions throughout the West, conditions can become quite severe during the late fall, winter and early spring. Elevations above 6,500 feet often receive significant amounts of snow during the winter, and access may be difficult or impossible in particular areas. These higher elevations occasionally receive snows as late as April or May. During mid-winter, it is not unusual for snow levels to descend as low as 3,000 feet elevation during particularly cold storms. Summer temperatures are quite comfortable, often staying in the 70° range during the day and dropping into the 50s or 60s at night. Afternoon and evening thunderstorms are typical from late June through September at elevations above 6,000 feet. These storms can be violent, and temperatures often drop as much as 20 degrees surrounding these events. These storms in particular often produce spectacular lightning shows and can be quite dangerous. Do not venture out during storms and take precautions to avoid being struck by lightning. If you are planning on visiting high elevation areas, it would be wise to check the weather forecast first.

Water

Water is one of the single most important items to carry afield in warm and arid climates. It is important to keep well hydrated. The best way to do this is to regularly drink water, regardless of thirst. Thirst is actually a relatively poor indicator of your need for water. The average person not engaged in strenuous activity should drink about 1 quart of water an hour (2 gallons in 8 hours) in temperatures exceeding 100°. Though some sport drinks are good hydrators, those with electrolytes, soft drinks, tea, alcohol, etc., should not be substituted for water.

Cholla

Hazardous Terrain

Much of Arizona can be difficult country to traverse. Rocky terrain is typical for much of the state, and it is not uncommon to encounter steep inclines, cliffs and precipitous canyons. Loose rocks or unstable ground can add significantly to the danger of any canyon edge or landscape. Care should be taken to avoid undue risk to personal safety and well-being in canyon country.

Adding to the hazards of hiking in Arizona—though more of an annoyance than a serious threat—are plants with thorns or spines. The most notorious of these is the "jumping" cholla (pronounced CHO-yah). Though many species of cactus can capture your attention quickly with a misplaced hand or step, none do so with more seeming enthusiasm and tenacity than the jumping cholla. When walking in cactus country, pay particular attention to where you place feet and hands. Often, a litter of fallen joints surrounds the base of a cactus and it is not uncommon for people and pets to be stabbed by these. Do not attempt to remove cactus segments from yourself or pets with your hands. A comb slid between the victim and the plant and then quickly pulled away from the victim is an effective way to remove cactus. Individual spines can then be removed by hand or with tweezers.

Things that Bite and Sting

Arizona is home to 15 species of venomous reptiles (13 rattlesnakes, Gila monster and coralsnake). That's more species of venomous reptiles than are found east of the Mississippi River! Though bites from rattlesnakes are not uncommon, deaths from encounters are rare.

Rattlesnakes can be encountered any warm day of the year, but for the most

Western Diamond-backed Rattlesnake

part reptiles are inactive during the cooler months (late November through early January).

When visiting rattlesnake country (particularly Arizona's middle and lower elevations), watch where you place your hands and feet. Keep in mind that most venomous animals are shy and retiring and go to great lengths to avoid conflicts and encounters with larger animals (this includes you).

Do not attempt to kill, harass, or interact with rattlesnakes or other venomous animals, as many bites are incurred in this manner. Gila monsters and coral-snakes only bite when handled and therefore should not be considered a threat, though they are capable of painful and dangerous bites.

Scorpions are seldom active during the day, and your chances of encountering one are slim unless camping or moving surface objects. Stings from most species are painful but not life-threatening.

Africanized bees are one of the few animals encountered that offer a genuine threat. Individual bees visiting flowers or buzzing by offer no threat, but those in or near hives are particularly easy to aggravate and care should be taken not to disturb them. ANY beehive encountered in the field should be considered to be inhabited by Africanized bees and avoided. These bees are easily agitated and can be very dangerous; they have caused several deaths to livestock, pets and people.

Visitors may encounter a variety of other wildlife and should take care not to approach or attempt to feed or interact with them. Keep wildlife wild—enjoy them at a safe distance.

OTHER SAFETY ISSUES

Hunting
Depending on the time of your visit, there may be hunts taking place for one or more species of wildlife. Arizona has one of the best hunter safety records in the nation. Regardless, care should be taken not to interfere with these activities or expose yourself to any undue risk. If you are afield during a hunt, wear brightly colored clothing such as orange or red. If opportunity allows, inform any hunters encountered of your presence and intentions.

There are many places to watch wildlife where restricted, limited, or no hunting is allowed, including national parks, monuments, memorials, national wildlife refuges, state parks and county parks.

Border Issues
Homeland security issues along the international border may affect the quality of your experience in this area. Illegal entry and smuggling are common activities in remote areas, and language barriers increase the potential risk to visitors.

Please be aware of your surroundings at all times and do not travel alone. Expect possible high-speed driving and law enforcement pursuits. Unattended vehicles can be damaged or stolen. Always let others know your expected route and destination. Report suspicious persons or activities to authorities.

Flash Floods/Monsoon Weather Issues

Summertime monsoon storms can be very violent. These storms, though typically short in duration, can drop significant amounts of rain. In addition to powerful winds, these storms are characterized by searing displays of lightning. It is wise to avoid outdoor activity during these events, or if caught outside, take shelter in your automobile or some other appropriate site. Normally dry washes or small creeks often become churning, muddy torrents in minutes during monsoon storms. These events are referred to as flash floods due to their sudden appearance and violent nature. An often confusing aspect of these floods is that it need not be raining at the place where the flood occurs; these floods are often the product of rains many miles away. Camping or lingering in washes should be avoided, especially during rainy weather. Travelers have died while attempting to cross flooded washes. Patience and caution are virtues that serve summer travelers well. When a flooded wash is encountered, often all that is required for a safe crossing is to wait for a short period for the water to recede. Flash floods typically occur in pulses, and deep, dangerous waters are often short-lived. When a flash flood is encountered, a short wait will often result in passable conditions.

Sandhill Cranes

Wildlife Viewing at Night

Most wildlife watchers go to bed early and get up at the crack of dawn to enjoy the early morning colors and wildlife activity. In fact most of the books written on watching wildlife advise that early morning and late day are the best times for wildlife watchers to be out and about. If you take this advice, at least in Arizona, you may be missing some of the best we have to offer, especially during the summer. Many species of wildlife such as bats, owls, moths, many frogs and toads, scorpions and others are completely nocturnal (only active at night). Because of our intense summer heat, many other species commonly seen during the day become seasonally nocturnal. Examples of seasonally nocturnal species are elk, coyote, fox, badger and many snakes. If you want to see nocturnal species at any time of the year, or you visit Arizona during the summer and want to see our seasonally nocturnal species, you should plan on staying up late. And if you want to see some of Arizona's most interesting species, nocturnal viewing is a must.

So, how do you find animals at night? Many nocturnal animals including snakes, scorpions, owls, elk, coyotes and others can best be viewed by "road riding." This process consists of driving slowly on remote roads in suitable habitat. In Arizona,

Elk

it is legal to "spotlight" animals (except during hunting season) but when you are in the vehicle, use only your headlights. After you spot the critter that you want a closer look at, move safely off the road, get out of the vehicle—then turn on your larger light and enjoy. This is an especially good method for viewing large numbers of elk as they feed in meadows during the hot summer months. In general, owls can be seen as they cross the road either chasing prey or trying to get away from your bright headlights. Be prepared to see snakes, especially during the monsoon evenings. Viewing is best done from a safe distance, unless you are an expert and know how to get close.

Those of you interested in the unusual might enjoy scorpion hunting! Find an area in the desert (creosote habitat is especially good for viewing scorpions) and walk out in the flats with a black light. Since scorpions glow yellow/green in the reflection of the black light, they are easy to find and can be approached. Watch them as they hunt and eat their insect prey.

Arizona is home to 28 species of bats. Get a little out of town and close to a strong light. Security lights around buildings and some remote street lights can be particularly productive because they attract flying insects, the main food source of most bats. Bats can be seen as they fly through the lighted areas eating insects. Some of Arizona's most unusual bats feed on the nectar of specific flowers, and they also enjoy the sugar water from hummingbird feeders. If you are in the foothill habitats of southeast Arizona from July through October, find someone with a hummingbird feeder and convince them to leave it out at night. Get in a comfortable chair and watch the feeder. About one to one and a half hours after dark, expect to see lesser long-nosed or Mexican long-tongued bats feeding at the feeder.

Remember when watching wildlife, especially at night, it is best to keep your distance and always be aware of your surroundings.

Outdoor Ethics

Though most of Arizona is public land (about 60%), there is a good deal of private land, including American Indian reservations. Care should be taken to respect these properties. Tribal lands can be accessed with a permit that is usually available through tribal governmental offices or sanctioned outlets like sporting goods stores. Permission will be needed for access to any privately-owned lands. Treat private lands with respect to keep access open to those who follow you.

Arizona has specific laws prohibiting the harassment of wildlife. Sometimes in our enthusiasm to get a better view or picture of wildlife, we unnecessarily frighten the animal. Care should be taken to avoid causing any animal undue stress by approaching it too close, chasing it, or keeping it away from young or water. For example, stopping near a meadow to observe elk feeding and causing them to move into cover would not be considered harassment;

however, pursuing them with an automobile or ATV to get a better look would be considered harassment. Think of the animal's well-being, and place it above your desire to see it or photograph it.

Lastly, who hasn't been afield soaking in the spectacular view or unspoiled scenery only to have their eye land on some discarded rubbish. No one enjoys seeing an otherwise pristine place marred by litter. Be sure and keep your recreation area clean; place your trash in an appropriate container or carry it out with you.

GENERAL VIEWING HINTS

Timing is everything! Most wildlife follow specific activity patterns, both seasonally and daily, and are seldom seen outside of these often rigid activity periods. These activity periods can shift depending on many factors such as weather, temperature or breeding period. For instance, during the hot summer months, javelina are active primarily at night (nocturnal). However, when winter temperatures turn cool, they become active during the day (diurnal). Many wildlife species are most active during the early morning and late afternoon/evening hours (crepuscular). This is especially true of deer, elk and many bird species. During crepuscular activity periods, it is not unusual to encounter wildlife species that are primarily nocturnal or diurnal. Many nocturnal wildlife species are best observed long after sundown or when it is truly dark, though some bats and other animals become active at sundown. Artificial lights might be necessary to see most nocturnal species of wildlife, but many species such as bats, raccoons and opossums frequent lighted areas in search of insects or other prey. Many reptiles, amphibians and rodents are primarily nocturnal, especially during the warm season. In contrast, most birds are readily observed throughout the day, despite being more active in the morning and evening.

Aside from planning your visit at the appropriate time of day, the time of year should also be taken into account. Many migratory birds such as waterfowl, sandhill cranes and raptor species are best observed in the southern portion of the state during the winter. These birds migrate to Arizona from all over North America to take advantage of the warm winters. During the spring and summer, several species of birds and other animals migrate north into the state to breed. Caracaras, white-winged doves and lesser long-nosed bats are examples of these. By timing your visit to activity peaks and patterns, both seasonally and daily, you can greatly increase your chances of seeing wildlife.

Keep in Mind . . .

There are probably natural areas where you live. If you are moved by nature during your Arizona trip, make time to get involved in your community's projects when you return home. Volunteer. Join a conservation organization. Get your children involved. Take a hike, plant a tree, or help with a cleanup project to expand your understanding of nature, lighten your spirit, enrich family ties, and most importantly, help preserve the world's wildlife for future generations.

How to Use This Guide

The sites featured in this book have been divided into five regions:

Canyonlands
Central Mountains
River and Desert
Sky Islands
White Mountains

Within each region, the sites are categorized into three types:

These are the most significant sites, and are the places you'll want to consider visiting if you have only a limited time. Their site narratives run four to six pages.

These are also important wildlife viewing sites. In some cases, the types of wildlife species that might be seen are more limited. Their site narratives run two pages.

The "other" sites are worth visiting when time is not a factor. They are often small and have limited parking. Please do not be quick to discount these sites as many are magnets for wildlife. Local site narratives are less than a page long.

As you glance through the pages of this guide, you will notice that each site narrative follows the same format. This should make it easy for you to compare sites and find important information.

Sprinkled throughout the book are "Species Notes" featuring highlighted species that you may wish to see during your visit.

The site name is the most common name attributed to the site. Sites are organized by regions (Canyonlands, Central Mountains, River and Desert, Sky Islands and White Mountains) and within each region they are organized by type (Premier, Great, Other).

★ Indicates type of site (Premier) and number on map

▲ Indicates type of site (Great) and number on map

● Indicates type of site (Other) and number on map

Description

Mentions some of the key sights and wildlife experiences at the site.

Wildlife to Watch

Gives specific information about the species you might expect to see, the best seasons for viewing and your chances of seeing them. Some natural history information is also provided.

Viewing Tips

Suggests where to see the species and ways to improve your chances of seeing them.

Trails

Features trail information at the site, including trail length, accessibility and difficulty notes.

Site Notes Gives information about the sites, such as the best times to visit the site, parking or entry fees, permit information or other specific tips.

Size Indicates approximates size of the site.*

Directions Gives driving directions to the site from the nearest town.

Nearest town Indicates nearest town to the site where visitors may find gas, dining, lodging, etc.*

Ownership Indicates who is responsible for owning or managing the site.*

Contact Provides the site manager's address and telephone number. Note that not all sites have a local office and telephone number. Whenever possible, a website address is provided.

Features A list of the types of amenities that are available at the site.

*Information not included in "Other" sites.

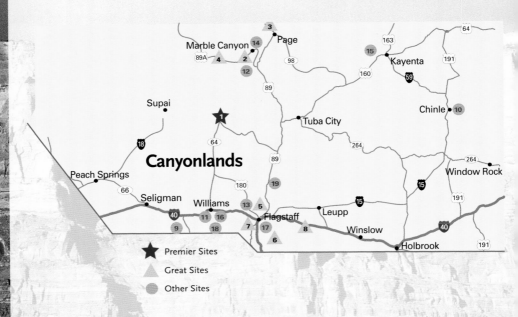

Canyonlands

The opportunity to view one of the seven natural wonders of the world, the Grand Canyon, lures visitors to this area throughout the year. But the passage of time and the forces of geology are dramatically displayed throughout the Canyonlands region, particularly at places like Canyon de Chelly, the Vermilion Cliffs and the Kaibab Plateau.

The colorful sedimentary rock formations so dramatically exposed along the Colorado River's course underlie most of the Canyonlands region. These rocks were formed tens of millions of years ago, when a vast ocean covered most of the western United States.

In this dry, often harsh country, the passages of time and weather are written on red rock cliffs and in sinuous canyons. Desert shrubs and grasses, or woodlands of pinyon pine and juniper, dominate the lowlands. Ponderosa pine and mixed-conifer forests generally grow above 7,000 feet.

PHOTO BY BRUCE D. TAUBERT

Canyon Wren

PHOTO BY BRIAN E. SMALL

Description

The significance and appeal of the Grand Canyon is not limited to spectacular vistas and fascinating geology. The park contains several major ecosystems and great biological diversity. It spans nearly 8,000 feet in elevation, from the Mohave Desert scrub regions along the Colorado River in the park's western end to the Kaibab Plateau's subalpine conifer forests of the North Rim. Its large size, relatively unfragmented and diverse habitat, and range of elevations and associated climates have made Grand Canyon National Park a valuable wildlife area. Over 1,500 species of plants, 355 birds, 89 mammals, 47 reptiles, 9 amphibians and 17 fish are found in the park.

Visiting the South Rim The South Rim of the Grand Canyon is open to visitors year-round. Canyon View Information Plaza is the park's visitor facility, with the Canyon View Visitor Center, a large bookstore and restrooms all within a short walk of Mather Point. Park your car and ride the free shuttle or walk the short trail from Mather Point. There are many overlooks accessible by car that offer spectacular views of the canyon. Desert View Drive (Highway 64) follows the canyon rim for 26 miles east of Grand Canyon Village to Desert View, the park's east entrance. Desert View Drive is open to private vehicles throughout the year. Hermit Road follows the rim for eight miles west from Grand Canyon Village to Hermits Rest. Hermit Road is closed to private vehicles much of the year, but the park runs a free shuttle bus to provide transportation to overlooks. Yavapai Point offers panoramic views of the canyon, including the Colorado River and Phantom Ranch.

Visiting the North Rim The North Rim of the Grand Canyon is open until winter weather conditions prevent travel on Highway 67 from Jacob Lake; it is

CANYONLANDS ■ *Grand Canyon National Park*

Premier
★ SITE ★

30 miles to the park's northern entrance and another 14 miles to the canyon rim. The North Rim, at an elevation approximately 1,000 feet higher than the South Rim, offers visitors a different experience than the South Rim. Crowds can be fewer, except at peak summer visitation, and vistas sweep across to the lower elevations of the south rim.

The North Rim Visitor Center offers park and regional information, maps, brochures, exhibits and a bookstore. Bright Angel Point is located a short, easy walk from the end of the entrance road to Grand Canyon Lodge and offers a classic view of the canyon. A paved, half-mile (round-trip) trail leads from the lodge, out the spine of the ridge, to the point.

Three developed viewpoints on the North Rim offer a sense of looking across the expanse of the canyon, rather than into its depths. Point Imperial and Cape Royal are reached via a winding scenic drive. Point Sublime, the western-most of the North Rim viewpoints, lies a rough, two-hour (one-way) drive away.

Wildlife to Watch

Three broad wildlife habitats exist within the park: the Colorado River corridor and inner canyon riparian areas, inner canyon desert uplands and the coniferous forests. Wildlife varies greatly in each habitat, and each offers unique viewing opportunities.

Riparian The diversity of vegetation along the riparian zone creates a corresponding variety of wildlife habitats. A total of 34 mammal species are found along the Colorado River corridor, including mule deer, bighorn sheep, coyote, ringtail, bats, spotted skunk, raccoon, bobcat and gray fox. Mountain lion are also present but are rarely seen. Of the 355 bird species recorded in the greater Grand Canyon region, 250 are found in the Colorado River corridor. Canyon treefrog, red-spotted and Woodhouse's toads are commonly encountered on the river's shores, and eastern collared lizard, common side-blotched lizard and tiger whiptail may be seen basking on rocks.

Desert Scrub In spring, summer and early fall, the south rim near Grand Canyon Village is one of the best sites in the world to view California condors. The cliffs along the inner canyon provide nesting sites for approximately 100 pairs of peregrine falcons. Fifty species of mammals, consisting mostly of rodents and bats, occur in this habitat. Numerous caves in the inner canyon provide roost sites for migratory and resident bats, including the unique spotted bat. Spring, summer and fall offer excellent opportunities to view bighorn sheep. Three species of rattlesnake are found within the canyon, and numerous lizards and other snakes inhabit the precipitous slopes. Brilliantly colored eastern collared lizards are undoubtedly the most gaudy of the lizards found in the canyon, while Gila monsters have been documented from the canyon's lower reaches. Common side-blotched lizards and tiger whiptails are the most commonly seen lizards in this habitat; common chuckwallas and desert spiny lizards haunt the boulder-strewn slopes and canyons. Though snakes are seldom seen in all habitats, the Grand Canyon rattlesnake is probably the most famous of the park's serpentine inhabitants.

Coniferous Forest The conifer forests provide habitat for 52 mammal species, including porcupine, red squirrel, rock squirrel and mule deer. A unique population of Abert's squirrel, the Kaibab squirrel, can be found on the north rim of the Grand Canyon. They differ from other Abert's squirrels in having dark undersides and a nearly all-white tail. Other mammals that may occur but are rarely observed include black bear, mountain lion and elk. Bird species that can be observed include northern goshawk, blue grouse, yellow-rumped and black-throated gray warblers, white-throated swift and canyon wren, along with the ever-present common raven. Reptiles include western skink (found only on the north rim), plateau lizard, greater short-horned lizard, eastern collared lizard, gopher snake and black-tailed rattlesnake.

Trails

The park has a significant trail system for all levels of recreationists. The Rim Trail follows the rim from Mather Point to Hermits Rest. The section of the Rim Trail between Pipe Creek Vista and Maricopa Point is paved. Unpaved portions of the trail, between Maricopa Point and Hermits Rest, are narrow and close to the edge of the canyon. Bicycles are not permitted on the Rim Trail.

Spotted Bat

PHOTO BY BRUCE D. TAUBERT

Premier
★ SITE ★

Site Notes Visitors should pay particular attention to posted park safety advisories. For viewing and photographing the canyon, the best light is early or late in the day. If you plan to see the canyon at sunrise or sunset, it is recommended that you be on the rim at least an hour before.

Size 1,218,375 acres

Directions From Williams: Take Hwy. 64 north to the Grand Canyon.
From Flagstaff: Take Hwy. 180 north, then right on Hwy. 64 to the Grand Canyon.
From Cameron: Take Hwy. 64 west to the Grand Canyon.

Nearest Town Tusayan

Ownership National Park Service

Contact 928-638-7888
www.nps.gov/grca/index.htm

Features restrooms, trash cans, trails, overlooks, interpretive signs, brochure/species list, visitor center, drinking water, bus/motorhome access, parking

Peregrine Falcon

PHOTO BY JACK CAFFERTY

Bighorn Sheep

PHOTO BY KENNETH H. MORGAN

Grand Canyon Rattlesnake

PHOTO BY RANDY BABB

Premier
★ SITE ★

Vermilion Cliffs Condor Viewing Site

A great place to view one of North America's most endangered birds

Vermilion Cliffs National Monument

PHOTO BY CHRIS PARRISH

Description

The California condor soars the skies of Arizona once again, thanks to a reintroduction effort that began here at Vermilion Cliffs in 1996. A condor-viewing kiosk at the west end of the monument invites visitors to look for these enormous black birds. From the kiosk, visitors are almost guaranteed to see condors soaring above the beautiful Vermilion Cliffs at any time of year. Viewing is best at mid- to late morning with the aid of binoculars or a spotting scope.

Wildlife to Watch

In addition to the California condor, look for peregrine falcon, prairie falcon and golden eagle, as well as a variety of reptiles and amphibians, such as gopher snake, Great Basin eastern collared lizard, common sagebrush lizard and greater short-horned lizard. Bighorn sheep, pronghorn, mountain lion and other mammals such as white-tailed antelope squirrel, rock squirrel, badger, ringtail and spotted skunk may also be present. The many cliffs and rock outcrops are home to white-throated swift and violet-green swallow.

Directions To the Condor Viewing Site/Kiosk: From Jacob Lake go east on Hwy. 89A down the switchbacks. Turn north on House Rock Valley Road (BLM Rd 1065) and travel 3 miles up to the viewing kiosk. From Page, travel south on Hwy. 89 to the Hwy. 89A turnoff to Lees Ferry/Jacob Lake. Go north on Hwy. 89A past Marble Canyon Lodge, Vermilion Cliffs Lodge and Cliff Dwellers Lodge. BLM Rd. 1065 is just past the snow chain-up area at the end of the valley. Just north of the junction of Hwy. 89A and BLM Rd. 1065 is a sign denoting entrance to monument.

Nearest Town Jacob Lake

Ownership Bureau of Land Management

Contact 435-688-3246
www.blm.gov/az/vermilion/vermilfctsht.htm

Features kiosk, parking

California Condor

PHOTO BY CHRIS PARRISH

Great
▲ SITE ▲

A kaleidoscope of colors where canyon meets river

Glen Canyon National Recreation Area

PHOTO BY BRUCE D. TAUBERT

Description

Striated red-orange cliffs and the opportunity to enjoy clear desert skies above sparkling blue water draw many visitors to this recreation area, which includes Lake Powell, a stretch of the Colorado River and miles of rocky desert country. Encompassing hundreds of miles from Lees Ferry in Arizona to the Orange Cliffs of southern Utah, the area offers scenic vistas, geologic wonders and a panorama of human history. Boating, fishing, swimming, backcountry hiking and four-wheel driving opportunities abound.

Wildlife to Watch

Wildlife may include bighorn sheep, small mammals such as desert cottontail, black-tail jackrabbit, cliff chipmunk, rock squirrel, coyote, gray fox, badger and ringtail, and birds of prey, including possible California condors. Waterfowl and gulls may also be observed, particularly at Lees Ferry during migration and winter. During spring and fall migration, birders may find good numbers of songbirds among the shade trees and orchard at the Lonely Dell Ranch Historic Site near the mouth of the Paria River and Lees Ferry. Both Cooper's hawk and Say's phoebe nest here, as do Lucy's warbler, yellow-breasted chat and Bewick's wren among the nearby tamarisk thickets. Area reptiles and amphibians include Great Basin rattlesnake, gopher snake, nightsnake, common kingsnake, eastern collared lizard, Mexican spadefoot, Woodhouse's toad and red-spotted toad.

Great
▲ SITE ▲

Trails

Agua Tierra Loop Trail ⅘-mile, easy trail, through cultivated gardens and desert landscapes; starts at Lake Powell Lodge and ends at Wahweap Visitor Contact Station.

Cathedral Wash Trail 1¼ miles one way, moderate difficulty, trailhead near Lees Ferry.

Numerous day hikes from various sites throughout the monument, ranging from easy to moderate difficulty. See website for additional information.

Site Notes	Fee site.
Size	1,250,000 acres
Directions	From Page, the main access is from various roads off Hwy. 89 or by boat. Access from the Utah side is from Hwy. 276 or by boat.
Nearest Town	Page
Ownership	National Park Service
Contact	928-608-6200 www.nps.gov/glca/
Features	restrooms, trash cans, trails, lookouts, interpretive signs, brochure/species list, drinking water, visitor center, boat ramps, parking

American Wigeon

PHOTO BY BRUCE D. TAUBERT

Great
▲ SITE ▲

Kaibab Plateau Parkway

PHOTO BY BRUCE D. TAUBERT

Description

A gentle, winding 44-mile drive through ponderosa pine, spruce fir and mountain meadows leads to a breathtaking view from the North Rim of the Grand Canyon. This National Scenic Byway, named by explorer John Wesley Powell, travels the Kaibab Plateau. The word "Kaibab" is derived from a Paiute word meaning "mountain lying down." The enormous plateau extends 45 miles east to west and 60 miles north to south, ending abruptly at the Grand Canyon.

Nestled in ponderosa pine forests at 7,925 feet elevation, the village of Jacob Lake offers a visitor center and other services. The town and nearby lake were named for Mormon missionary and explorer Jacob Hamblin. Jacob Lake Inn, the Kaibab Plateau Visitor Center and Jacob Lake Campground are near the State Hwy. 67 turnoff for the North Rim of the Grand Canyon.

Wildlife to Watch

The Kaibab Plateau is home to the densest population of northern goshawks in the United States. This is also an excellent place to see mule deer and the Kaibab squirrel. This striking squirrel has a contrasting black belly and white tail, and is found only here and on nearby Mount Trumbull. Merriam's turkey, blue grouse, Williamson's and red-naped sapsuckers, American three-toed woodpecker, Clark's nutcracker, evening grosbeak, red crossbill, pine siskin, Cassin's finch and Grace's warbler are a few of the many birds to be seen here.

CANYONLANDS ■ *Kaibab Plateau Parkway*

Great
▲ SITE ▲

A California condor sighting is also possible during the spring through fall months, as the condors forage for carrion on the plateau.

Site Notes	Winter weather may cause closure of State Hwy. 67 at Jacob Lake. Contact ADOT at the website below before traveling.
Size	parkway is a 44-mile route
Directions	The parkway starts at the junction of State Hwy. 67 and U.S. 89A at Jacob Lake.
Nearest Town	Jacob Lake
Ownership	U.S.D.A. Forest Service
Contact	928-643-7395; www.fs.fed.us/r3/kai/about/index.shtml
Features	(at Jacob Lake) restrooms, trash cans, interpretive signs, brochure/bird species list, drinking water

Northern Goshawk

PHOTO BY BRUCE D. TAUBERT

CANYONLANDS ■ Kaibab Plateau Parkway

Great ▲ SITE ▲

5

Lamar Haines Memorial Wildlife Area

Mammals and birds gather around springs in a scenic mountain meadow

Lamar Haines Memorial Wildlife Area

PHOTO BY GEORGE ANDREJKO

Description

A window into the past, this old homestead on the south slope of the San Francisco Peaks comprises two springs in a small, scenic mountain meadow. The springs form a small creek and pond which, along with large ponderosa pine, fir and aspen trees, provide excellent habitat for migrating songbirds and cavity-nesting birds. Follow the old road to the homestead, which provides easy access to this walk-in viewing area.

Wildlife to Watch

Visitors have a good probability of seeing elk and mule deer, Abert's squirrel, golden-mantled ground squirrel, greater short-horned lizard and plateau lizard. It is also an excellent place to observe mixed-conifer songbirds. Year-round resident birds can include Lewis's, downy, hairy and American three-toed wood-peckers; also Steller's jay, mountain chickadee, red-breasted and white-breasted nuthatches and brown creeper. Additional spring and summer breeding birds include Cordilleran flycatcher, western tanager, dark-eyed junco, and occasionally evening grosbeak and red crossbill. Go early in the day and move quietly for a good chance to see wildlife.

Trails

A rugged, 1½-mile trail to the homestead begins at the gate and goes to the right; another trail goes straight, following a narrow meadow into the National Forest.

Great
▲ SITE ▲

Site Notes Winter snows will close access to this area.

Size 160 acres

Directions From Flagstaff travel northwest on Hwy. 180 for 7 miles to the Snowbowl Road (FS Rd 516). Turn north and go 4½ miles to the parking area at the wildlife area entrance.

Nearest Town Flagstaff

Ownership Arizona Game and Fish Department

Contact 928-774-5045; www.azgfd.gov

Features trail, parking

Mule Deer

PHOTO BY KENNETH H. MORGAN

Great
▲ SITE ▲

6

Mormon Lake-Doug Morrison Overlook

Best opportunity to see wintering bald eagles in Arizona

Mormon Lake

PHOTO BY GEORGE ANDREJKO

Description

Mormon Lake is the largest natural lake in Arizona—though water levels vary dramatically from year to year, and in drought conditions the lake has been known to go completely dry. Mormon Mountain looms on the west side of the lake. The lake was formed in a natural depression created as the limestone of the Kaibab formation dissolved. Lava flows surround this depression and the lava escarpment of Anderson Mesa rims State Hwy. 3 on the lake's north side.

Beautiful scenery and abundant wildlife viewing throughout the year draw visitors here. At 7,300 feet in elevation, the area offers a blend of habitats, including wetlands, open water, grassland, coniferous forests and cliffs. An overlook provides a prime observation point for scanning the vast lakebed and native grasslands.

South of Mormon Lake, visitors see long expanses of ponderosa pine forest, as well as patches of Gambel oak, pinyon pine and juniper. Butterflies bring flashes of color to the area, which also features historic sites from early Mormon pioneers. One of these, the water pumphouse on the west side of Mormon Lake, was established by the Mormon dairy in 1878.

Wildlife to Watch

The lake supports one of the largest concentrations of wintering bald eagles in the state—the highest number of bald eagles ever recorded at one place in Arizona was counted here in 1995 (65 eagles). The overlook at Mormon Lake has interpretive signage about the eagles. In addition to the eagles and osprey,

Great
▲ SITE ▲

there are excellent opportunities to see elk, pronghorn and a variety of water-fowl and songbirds. Watch on the nearby fences and other exposed perches for mountain bluebirds. During the fall, the overlook provides an excellent opportunity to view migrating raptors. Visitors should watch for plateau lizards or eastern collared lizards basking on the rocks.

Audubon
IMPORTANT
BIRD AREAS

Site Notes Be cautious of elk crossing the road, as well as bicyclists along the route.

Size 9 square miles

Directions From Flagstaff, travel southeast on Forest Highway 3 (FH3, also known as Lake Mary Road) for 21 miles to Mormon Lake. Forest Road 90 circles around the west side of the lake and returns to FH3. The Doug Morrison Overlook is along FH3 on the NE side of the lake.

Nearest Town Flagstaff and Mormon Lake Village

Ownership U.S.D.A. Forest Service, Coconino National Forest

Contact 928-527-3600
www.fs.fed.us/r3/coconino/recreation/mormon_lake/index.shtml

Features restrooms, trash cans, overlooks, interpretive signs, brochure/bird species list, bus/motorhome access, boat ramps, parking, picnic area

Bald Eagles   PHOTO BY TOM VEZO

Great
▲ SITE ▲

7

Pumphouse Greenway/Kachina Wetlands

Man-made wetlands close to Flagstaff; elk in summer and many birds year-round

Pumphouse Greenway/Kachina Wetlands

PHOTO BY GEOFFREY GROSS

Description

Pumphouse Greenway and Kachina Wetlands offer unique, wetland-wildlife watching opportunities in an easy-to-access, urban setting near Flagstaff. Pumphouse Greenway is a rare, high-elevation wet meadow, where spring-fed sheet flows of water lead to a meandering stream through Pumphouse Wash. Part of Coconino County Parks and Recreation's Open Space, Pumphouse Greenway is a nationally recognized "Five-Star Collaborative Conservation Project."

Kachina Wetlands is a wastewater treatment facility maintained by Kachina Village Improvement District, just up the hill from Pumphouse Greenway, where wastewater treatment reservoirs and surrounding vegetation attract both birds and birders. The sites are within a mile of each other, so visit both areas together to view wildlife in a diverse range of habitats.

Wildlife to Watch

At Pumphouse Greenway, visitors can see everything from grassland birds to waterbirds to forest birds in one place. In the meadow, Brewer's and vesper sparrows are fairly common seasonally; great blue heron forage for small fish and frogs; large choruses of red-winged blackbirds sing from the bulrush; and mallard, northern shoveler, green-winged teal, northern pintail, gadwall and American wigeon are commonly viewed in the ponds in and around the meadow. Along the Pumphouse Wash nature trail, visitors may encounter western and mountain bluebirds, blue grosbeak, broad-tailed hummingbird, belted kingfisher, flycatchers, phoebes, five different species of swallows and the occasional Lewis's woodpecker. In late summer, large herds of elk congregate in the wet meadow, attracting hundreds of wildlife watchers.

Constructed wetlands and wastewater treatment ponds like those at Kachina Wetlands are hotspots for large numbers of waterbirds, as well as the occasional rare bird. Highlights include wintering bald eagle, osprey, eared grebe, Virginia rail, sora, phalarope, yellowleg, long-billed curlew, American avocet and numerous species of ducks. Twilight visits may offer glimpses of elk, mule deer, coyote, western chorus frog and several bat species.

Trails

Coconino County Parks and Recreation maintains two nature trails at Pumphouse Greenway, accessed from the parking lot. The Floating Trail is a short (⅛-mile) easy trail with a floating bridge that crosses a small pond. The Pumphouse Greenway Nature Trail is a ¾-mile round-trip, easy trail with wildlife viewing blinds, benches and four educational displays.

Kachina Village Improvement District maintains trails around the ponds at Kachina Wetlands. The trails are wide and well-traveled and weave around the treatment ponds throughout the wetlands.

Site Notes	Please respect the privacy of private landowners surrounding these sites by staying on designated trails. Please do not enter the wet meadow to approach the elk.
Size	Pumphouse Greenway is 129 acres; Kachina Wetlands are approximately 5 acres
Directions	Travel I-17 to exit 333, 5 miles south of Flagstaff and turn west. Raymond County Park is immediately to the north on Tovar Trail. The linear parkland extends from the meadow west to Harrenburg Wash, near Kachina Village Utility. To get to Kachina Wetlands from Pumphouse Greenway, continue north on Tovar Trail 1⅕ miles; the wetlands are on the north side of the road near its dead end.
Nearest Town	Flagstaff
Ownership	Pumphouse Greenway: Coconino County Parks and Recreation; Kachina Wetlands: Kachina Village Improvement District
Contact	928-679-8025 (Coconino County Parks and Recreation) 928-525-1775 (Kachina Village Improvement District)
Features	restroom open May 1 through October 1, trash cans, trails, bus/motorhome access, parking, picnic tables, benches, wildlife viewing blinds (not enclosed)

Great
▲ SITE ▲

Raymond Ranch Wildlife Area

PHOTO BY GEORGE ANDREJKO

CANYONLANDS ▪ Raymond Ranch Wildlife Area

Description

The Raymond Ranch Wildlife Area was a working ranch before 1942, and today it offers the opportunity to view pronghorn, elk, mule deer and buffalo. Tucked away in the grasslands at the foot of Anderson Mesa, a trail leads to a unique view of the San Francisco Peaks, especially impressive when the peaks are snow-covered.

Also of interest are earth cracks in the Kaibab limestone throughout the area; an interpretive sign highlighting earth cracks is along the trail. These cracks often reveal themselves as only small openings on the surface but can be quite deep and extensive.

Sunrise and sunset are magical times on these grasslands, and the views can be spectacular but be prepared for rapid weather changes and winds. There are few times when the wind is not blowing on Raymond Ranch.

Wildlife to Watch

Watch for pronghorn and elk as you drive south along the Buffalo Range Road from I-40; pronghorn are often seen in the first two miles. Look for elk where the road crosses Anderson Canyon, especially in the early morning or late afternoon. Drive the east road, which intersects the Buffalo Range Road 50 feet north of the second cattle guard for the chance to see the buffalo herd. The east road requires a high-clearance vehicle.

Look for Gunnison's prairie dogs along the Buffalo Range Road at the first cattle

Great
▲ SITE ▲

guard. The burrows are always visible but prairie dogs hibernate and are not visible from November to March. Burrowing owls also nest in this prairie dog town and are active from June to September. On the west side of the Buffalo Range Road, 1⅓ miles north of the Anderson Canyon Crossing, look for another Gunnison's prairie dog town. During spring and fall, ferruginous hawks and golden eagles are often seen hunting in the area. In the evenings, numerous bats can be seen flying among the canyons and drinking at waterholes. Reptiles in the area include the eastern collared lizard, common side-blotched lizard, greater short-horned lizard, gopher snake and the prairie rattlesnake.

Trails

From the headquarters, follow the interpretive signs around the 1⅓-mile loop trail. A steep trail leads to a view of the San Francisco Peaks.

Site Notes	Heavy rainfall during summer monsoons make the Buffalo Range Road nearly impassable. Where the road crosses Anderson Canyon, (4 miles south of I-40) the canyon may be flowing water several feet deep, which prohibits crossing by even 4WD vehicles.
Size	14,000 acres
Directions	Go east of Flagstaff on I-40 to Exit #225 (Buffalo Range Road). Drive south from I-40 for 9 miles.
Nearest Town	Flagstaff
Ownership	Arizona Game and Fish Department/Arizona State Land Department
Contact	928-774-5045; www.azgfd.govs/outdoor_recreation/wildlife_area_raymond_ranch.shtml
Features	restrooms, trash cans, trails, lookouts, interpretive signs, brochures/species list, drinking water, parking, five primitive campsites

Buffalo   PHOTO BY BRUCE D. TAUBERT

Great
▲ SITE ▲

Big Black Mesa Loop

9

Description

Roll down the windows to enjoy the scent of pinyon-juniper woodland along this 21-mile loop drive on Forest Road 573. The road follows the old Peavine Railroad grade in Limestone Canyon, passing an old limestone kiln.

Wildlife to Watch

Mule deer, javelina, coyote and birds of prey such as red-tailed hawk, golden eagle and American kestrel can be seen. Pronghorn may be in the open grasslands, along with lark sparrow, horned lark, and western and eastern meadowlarks. Common pinyon-juniper birds include gray and ash-throated flycatchers, Cassin's and western kingbirds, gray vireo, pinyon and western scrub-jays, juniper titmouse, bushtit, spotted and canyon towhees, rufous-crowned and black-chinned sparrows and Scott's oriole.

Directions From Paulden, go north on U.S. 89 for 7 miles to mile post 344; turn west on FR 573 (Bullock Road) and continue for 21 miles, returning to U.S. 89 approximately 2 miles south of Ash Fork.

Contact U.S.D.A. Forest Service, Prescott National Forest; 928-443-8000; www.fs.fed.us/outdoors/naturewatch/arizona/wildlife/big-black-mesa/index.shtml

Features overlooks

Canyon de Chelly National Monument

10

Description

The stark cliffs and deep gorges of this monument, one of the longest continually inhabited landscapes in North America, almost seem to vibrate with layers of history and memory. The canyon consists of four main gorges, with many side ravines branching eastward from the town of Chinle into the Defiance Plateau. Many cultural resources, including distinctive architecture, artifacts and rock imagery, are found in Canyon de Chelly, which continues to sustain a community of Navajo people who plant crops and maintain sheep and goats in the canyon.

Wildlife to Watch

Golden eagles can be seen here, along with turkey vulture and peregrine falcon. Seasonal migratory songbirds can be found among the cottonwoods and dense Russian olive stands near the canyon mouth. The pinyon juniper woodlands along the rim are frequented by pinyon and western scrub-jays, juniper titmouse, bushtit, Bewick's wren and white-breasted nuthatch. In summer, look for ash-throated flycatcher, western and Cassin's kingbirds, black-throated gray warbler, and gray and plumbeous vireos. Reptiles and amphibians in the area include the Hopi race of prairie rattlesnake, glossy snake, eastern collared lizard, ornate tree lizard, many-lined skink, red-spotted toad and Woodhouse's toad.

CANYONLANDS ■ Other Sites

Other sites

Trails

Rugged trails; one self-guided, others require guides.

Directions Go three miles east of Chinle on Route 7.

Contact National Park Service; 928-674-5500; www.nps.gov/cach/

Features restrooms, trash cans, trails, overlooks, interpretive signs, brochure/species list, visitor center, drinking water, bus/motorhome access, parking

Coleman Lake   11

Description

This small lake and wetland amid ponderosa pines have been improved to create island and water channels for anglers. Fall foliage can be outstanding, framing good views of Bill Williams Mountain.

Wildlife to Watch

Look for waterbirds, belted kingfisher and killdeer. Elk, mule deer, golden-mantled ground squirrel, Abert's squirrel and Merriam's turkey are common around the lake, and bald eagle winter here. Common resident birds in the pine forest such as Steller's jay, mountain chickadee, pygmy nuthatch, northern flicker, hairy woodpecker and dark-eyed junco are joined in summer by broad-tailed hummingbird, plumbeous vireo, yellow-rumped and Grace's warblers, violet-green swallow and chipping sparrow. Greater short-horned lizard and terrestrial gartersnake can be found around the lake.

Site Notes The road is usually closed by snow from January through March.

Directions From Williams, take FR 173 (Perkinsville Road) south for 7⅓ miles to Forest Road 108. Then go west 2 miles to Coleman Lake.

Contact U.S.D.A Forest Service, Kaibab National Forest; 928-635-5600

Features no facilities on site

House Rock Wildlife Area   12

Description

A herd of buffalo—one of only two herds managed by the State of Arizona—wanders the pinyon-juniper and desert scrub of this 60,000-acre wildlife area. House Rock Valley lies along the eastern edge of the Kaibab Plateau, offering vistas of Marble Canyon in Grand Canyon National Park. The wildlife area also borders the Saddle Mountain Wilderness to the southwest.

Wildlife to Watch

The buffalo range freely over the wildlife area and the neighboring Kaibab Plateau and are not always visible from the road. You may also see mule deer and pronghorn, desert cottontail, black-tail jackrabbit, cliff chipmunk, white-tailed antelope squirrel, coyote, gray fox, spotted skunk, loggerhead shrike, Say's phoebe, horned lark, sage and black-throated sparrows, various birds of prey, and maybe even California condor flying over from the

Other sites

Vermilion Cliffs. Reptiles include the Great Basin rattlesnake, gopher snake and eastern collared lizard.

Directions From Marble Canyon, go west on Hwy. 89A for 16 miles to the ranch road (FS Rd. 455/BLM Rd. 8910). Go south 22 miles to the information kiosk. From Jacob Lake proceed east about 20 miles on Hwy. 89A to FS Rd 455/BLM Rd. 8910.

Contact Arizona Game and Fish Department; 928-774-5045; www.azgfd.gov

Features brochure/species list

Kendrick Park Watchable Wildlife Trail 13

Description

On the road to the South Rim of the Grand Canyon, 2,000-acre Kendrick Park is a large meadow surrounded by ponderosa pine and aspen. The trail offers breathtaking views of the San Francisco Peaks, Kendrick Park and Kendrick Mountain.

Wildlife to Watch

Mammals include pronghorn, mule deer, elk, coyote, badger and Abert's squirrel. Steller's jay, mountain and western bluebirds, mountain chickadee, violet-green swallow, hairy woodpecker and red-tailed hawk are relatively easy to see here. Reptiles include eastern collared lizard, greater short-horned lizard, plateau lizard and gopher snake.

Trails

The site offers two loop trails, up to 1½ miles. One has universal accessibility and both trails have interpretive displays.

Directions The trail is adjacent to U.S. Hwy. 180, approximately 20 miles north of Flagstaff on the southern end of Kendrick Park.

Contact U.S.D.A. Forest Service, Coconino National Forest; 928-527-3600; www.fs.fed.us/r3/coconino/recreation/peaks/kendrick-watchable.shtml

Features restrooms, bus/motorhome access, interpretive signs, trails, brochure/species list, parking

Navajo Bridge 14

Description

Historic Navajo Bridge spans Marble Canyon in a graceful silvery arch approximately 470 feet above the Colorado River. For many years the only crossing of the Colorado River for 600 miles, it now serves as a pedestrian bridge providing excellent views of the canyon.

Wildlife to Watch

The California condor can be viewed at fairly close range, on cliffs below and flying over or under the bridge. You may also see turkey vulture, peregrine falcon and other birds of prey. The parking lot area is home to white-tailed antelope squirrel and rock squirrel, while the nearby cliffs and canyon walls harbor rock and canyon wrens. In the surrounding area see pronghorn, mule deer, coyote, gray fox, badger, raccoon and black-tail jackrabbit. Area reptiles and amphibians include Great Basin rattlesnake, gopher snake, nightsnake, common kingsnake and eastern collared lizard.

Site Notes An interpretive center is open from April to October.

Directions From Marble Canyon, take Hwy. 89 to the bridge. From Page, take Hwy. 89 south, to Hwy. 89A west to the river.

Contact National Park Service, Navajo Bridge Interpretive Center; 928-355-2319

Features restrooms, trash cans, overlooks, interpretive signs, visitor center, parking, Navajo vendors

Navajo National Monument   15

Description

High on the Shonto Plateau, overlooking the Tsegi Canyon system in the Navajo Nation, the Navajo National Monument comprises 600 acres and preserves three of the most intact cliff dwellings of the ancestral puebloan people (Hisatsinom). Today the Navajo people call these ancient ones "Anasazi."

Wildlife to Watch

Varied habitats within the canyon include species such as mule deer, coyote, mountain lion, desert cottontail and black-tailed jackrabbit. Birders hiking the trails will find a wide variety of birds, including turkey vulture, red-tailed hawk, American kestrel, gray flycatcher, western and mountain bluebirds, juniper titmouse, mountain chickadee, bushtit and Cassin's kingbird. Reptiles in the area include eastern collared lizard, common lesser earless lizard, common side-blotched lizard, ornate tree lizard, gopher snake and prairie rattlesnake.

Trails

Four trails from 1–17 miles in length. The 1-mile Sandal trail is accessible to wheelchairs. The guided hikes to Betatakin/Talastima and Keet Seel/Kawestima are recommended only for experienced and fit hikers.

Site Notes Rangers guide visitors on free tours of the cliff dwellings.

Directions From Kayenta, go 22 miles south on U.S.Highway 160 to AZ Hwy. 564 (Black Mesa Junction, then nine miles north).The monument is in the Navajo Nation in northern Arizona.

Contact National Park Service; 928-672-2700; www.nps.gov/nava/

Features restrooms, trash cans, trails, lookouts, interpretive signs, visitor center, drinking water, bus/motorhome access, parking, campgrounds, picnic area

Sunflower Flat Wildlife Area 16

Description

This beautiful 160-acre marsh offers the opportunity to see waterfowl and shorebirds in wet years. This currently undeveloped site is close to Garland Prairie and White Horse Lake.

Wildlife to Watch

At this ephemeral wetland, wildlife species vary based on water levels. With abundant water, the area resembles a shallow lake, and ducks such as bufflehead and common merganser can be found during spring, summer, and fall. Osprey and other birds of prey frequent the area during these months. Bald eagles can be found during winter months. During times with less precipitation, dabbling ducks such as northern shoveler, northern pintail, gadwall and cinnamon teal, and waterbirds such as great blue heron, white-faced ibis and American avocet frequent the area. In drier times, birds of prey such as red-tailed hawk and northern harrier can be found, as well as elk, pronghorn and mule deer. Reptiles and amphibians that may be found include greater short-horned and plateau lizards, gopher snake, Arizona black rattlesnake, Arizona toad, canyon and Arizona treefrogs.

Directions From Williams, go southeast on FR 141 about 5 miles to FR 109. Take this south about 3 miles to FR 14. Go south and west about 1 mile and look for unmarked road on left. Sunflower Flat is about ½ mile down this road.

Contact Arizona Game and Fish Department; 928-774-5045

Features no facilities on site

Upper and Lower Lake Mary 17

Description

Surrounded by ponderosa pine, Upper and Lower Lake Mary were developed to provide drinking water to nearby Flagstaff. Upper Lake Mary is popular with powerboats and water-skiers, while Lower Lake Mary offers a picnic area handy for enjoying lunch, sitting and observing wildlife or watching anglers try their luck.

Wildlife to Watch

Visitors can see many different species of waterfowl and shorebirds as well as mule deer, elk, cliff chipmunk, golden-mantled ground squirrel and Abert's squirrel along the trails. Bald eagle are frequently observed around the lake, particularly during winter. In recent years, a pair of breeding bald eagles has nested here. Other breeding birds of prey in the area include osprey and red-tailed hawk. An excellent spot to view breeding osprey is the Osprey Overlook along FH 3 adjacent to Upper Lake Mary. Visitors may encounter small reptiles or amphibians such as Arizona treefrog, Arizona toad, tiger salamander, many-lined skink, plateau lizard, terrestrial gartersnake, gopher snake and even Arizona black rattlesnake.

Trails

Several short, easy trails lead from the picnic area to the edge of the lake. Sandy's Canyon trail, a 1-mile section of easy trail that joins with the Arizona Trail, is about 2 miles west of the Lower Lake Mary picnic area.

Directions From Flagstaff, travel southeast on Forest Highway 3 for 8 miles past mile marker 338. Lower Lake Mary picnic area will be on the right. Typically during the winter months the gate to the picnic area will be closed.

Contact U.S.D.A. Forest Service, Coconino National Forest; 928-774-1147; www.fs.fed.us/r3/coconino/recreation/mormon_lake/lowermary-boat.shtml

Features restrooms, trash cans, trails, overlook, bus/motorhome access, boat ramps, parking

White Horse Lake-Pine Flat Route   18

Description

This 50-mile auto loop through ponderosa pine and oak habitat has several wildlife viewing areas and two lakes—White Horse and J.D. Lakes—where wildlife can be seen. White Horse Lake is a popular recreation area which has all facilities.

Wildlife to Watch

Mule deer, elk and Merriam's turkey are found in the area during spring. Bald eagle are common in the winter, and osprey and great blue heron nest at both lakes in the summer. You can also see violet-green and tree swallows, double-crested cormorant and a wide variety of waterfowl. During the summer, purple martin and violet-green swallow frequently forage over the lakes. Birds in the surrounding forests include broad-tailed hummingbird, western wood-pewee, plumbeous vireo, western bluebird, white-breasted and pygmy nuthatches and dark-eyed junco.

Directions From Williams, take Forest Road 173 south for 9 miles. Turn east on Forest Road 110, continue 7⅞₀ miles to White Horse Lake Road (Forest Road 109). To continue the loop return to FS 110, go 4 miles, follow signs to J.D. Lake, just behind the junction with Forest Road 105. Continue 8 miles to Pine Flat, where the road becomes Forest Road 354; continue straight 7 miles from Pine Flat and return to Williams.

Contact U.S.D.A. Forest Service, Kaibab National Forest; 928-635-5600; www.fs.fed.us/r3/kai/recreation/fishing/whitehorse.shtml

Features restrooms, trash cans, bus/motorhome access, interpretive displays (at lakes)

Wupatki National Monument

Description

Wupatki National Monument protects 56 square miles of high desert directly west of the Little Colorado River and the Navajo Reservation. Wupatki was the tallest, largest and perhaps the richest and most influential pueblo for a brief period 800 years ago.

Wildlife to Watch

Pronghorn, mule deer, antelope ground squirrel and black-tailed jackrabbit can be found here. Common birds include the western kingbird, rock wren, black-throated sparrow and greater roadrunner. Noisy flocks of pinyon jay can often be found in the nearby pinyon juniper woodlands, along with juniper titmouse, bushtit and hairy woodpecker. A wide array of seasonal migratory birds may be seen. Reptiles include eastern collared lizard, plateau lizard, greater short-horned lizard, striped plateau lizard, nightsnake, glossy snake, striped whipsnake, milksnake, gopher snake and the Hopi race of prairie rattlesnake.

Trails

This site offers three separate ½-mile trails to view pueblos and wildlife.

Directions From Flagstaff, take U.S. 89 north for 12 miles; turn right at sign for Sunset Crater Volcano-Wupatki National Monuments. The Visitor Center is 21 miles from this junction.

Contact National Park Service; 928-679-2365; www.nps.gov/wupa/

Features restrooms, trash cans, trails, lookouts, interpretive signs, brochure/species list, visitor center, drinking water, bus/motorhome access, parking, photo blinds

California Condor

California condor population declines in Arizona started in the late 1800s. This decline coincided with the settlement of the West and causes included toxins, shootings, specimen collecting and habitat encroachment. The last condor sighting in Arizona occurred in 1924. By the mid-1900s, the condors' range had shrunk to a small region in California. By 1982, only 22 condors remained in the world and the population was close to extinction.

The public and private sector intervened by capturing the remaining wild birds and starting a captive-breeding program. Captive breeding succeeded, and a coalition of public and private interests began releasing condors back into remote areas of California in 1992 and northern Arizona in 1996. In 2002, a third condor release program was initiated in Baja California, Mexico.

Condor recovery efforts have proven successful, with condor numbers increasing to almost 300 birds by 2007. Captive-reared condors are successfully breeding in the wild. Lead poisoning and trash ingestion have been identified as obstacles to the condors' recovery. Project cooperators are working hard to overcome these management issues. Their efforts, combined with support from the public, will hopefully lead to the future delisting of this endangered species.

California condors are the largest free-flying bird in Arizona, with a 9.5 foot wingspan and average weight of 20 pounds. Condors can fly up to 50 miles per hour and travel 200 miles in one day. They live up to 60 years in the wild. Pairs mate for life, first breed at 5-7 years of age, produce only one chick every other year, and share incubation and chick rearing duties. Condors eat 10% of their body weight at one time, but only need to eat 1-2 times per week. They are opportunistic scavengers that find food by sight, not smell.

Where to See Condors in Arizona

Spring through fall: South Rim of the Grand Canyon, soaring or perched on a rock between the El Tovar Hotel and Lookout Studio

Spring and fall: Navajo Bridge in Marble Canyon on U.S. Highway 89A

Year-round, but especially in winter: Vermilion Cliffs release site viewing area, three miles north of U.S. Highway 89A on BLM Road 1065

On the Web

Arizona Game and Fish Department's condor Web page: azgfd.gov/condor

The Peregrine Fund: peregrinefund.org

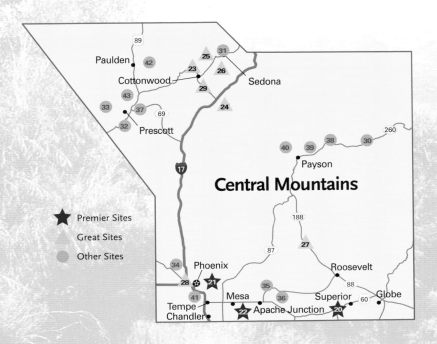

Premier Sites
Great Sites
Other Sites

Central Mountains

Geologists characterize Arizona's Central Mountains region as a transition zone because the area is sandwiched between the Colorado Plateau geological region to the north and the Basin and Range geological region to the south. The Central Mountains region is comprised of forested mountain ranges and gentle valleys.

Meandering waterways such as the Verde River draw birds and animals to their lush banks. Oak and pinyon-juniper woodlands, open grasslands and agave and yucca give this region its unique character, along with the stately and unmistakable saguaro cactus.

PHOTO BY ARIZONA STATE PARKS

Arid plants from around the world; great butterfly and bird viewing opportunities

Gila Woodpecker

PHOTO BY CINDY MARPLE

Description

Only one hour east of Phoenix and two hours from Tucson, the 1,075-acre Boyce Thompson Arboretum is among Arizona's premier watchable wildlife spots—in fact, it was among the first Important Bird Areas designated in the Grand Canyon State by the Audubon Society. Spring and fall weekend guided tours teach visitors to identify birds, and summertime tours include the popular "Learn Your Lizards" outing and guided butterfly and dragonfly walks.

The Arboretum is Arizona's oldest and largest botanical garden. With 4,400-foot Picketpost Mountain dominating the southern horizon, a combination of panoramic desert vistas, trails and desert plants from around the world welcome visitors. At an elevation of 2,400 feet, native Sonoran Desert vegetation is displayed in a Cactus Garden, while other attractions include a Heritage Rose Garden, Australian Forest, demonstration gardens and an Herb Garden. Queen Creek, an intermittent desert stream and the Arboretum's irrigated gardens and protected grounds provide a haven for local wildlife. More than 300 species of mammals, birds, reptiles and amphibians have been found at the Arboretum over the years.

CENTRAL MOUNTAINS ■ *Boyce Thompson Arboretum State Park*

Premier
★ SITE ★

Adjacent to the Arboretum is the scenic Picketpost Mansion, the 1920s winter home of mining magnate and philanthropist William Boyce Thompson, who founded his namesake Arboretum in 1924. The Smith Interpretive Center on the Arboretum grounds was built of locally quarried stone in 1925 and is on the National Register of Historic Places. Special events throughout the year include the Arboretum's unique salute to a signature migratory bird species: "Bye-Bye Buzzards" day in the fall and the "Welcome Back Buzzards" day each spring. Seasonal plant sales, a live music festival, fall color celebration on Thanksgiving weekend, Australia Day and the herb festival are among other events.

Described as a 350-acre living classroom, the Arboretum offers lizard walks, the Main Trail guided tour, landscaping classes, edible and medicinal desert plant walks, photography classes, wildflower identification and much more.

Wildlife to Watch

More than 230 bird and 72 species of mammals, reptiles and amphibians have been documented as either permanent and/or migratory Arboretum residents. These include Costa's and broad-billed hummingbirds, brown-crested flycatcher, black and Say's phoebes, cactus and canyon wrens, ruby-crowned kinglet, Gambel's quail, gilded flicker, curve-billed thrasher, and black-throated sparrow. The extensive irrigated areas of native and exotic trees and shrubs provide food and shelter for countless winter visitors and migratory species, including such rarities such rufous-backed robin and varied thrush.

Other wildlife includes the rock squirrel, Harris' antelope squirrel and desert cottontail. Snakes, tortoises and toads usually venture forth at dawn or dusk. Lizards such as the desert spiny lizard may be seen basking in the sun during the day. Other regularly encountered lizards include tiger whiptail, greater earless, common side-blotched and ornate tree lizards. Seeking shelter during the heat, many of the Arboretum's free-roaming inhabitants are not always evident during the day. Abundant but often unseen insects, spiders and scorpions are also part of the Arboretum's natural ecosystem. Two native fish, the Gila topminnow and desert pupfish, are in Ayer Lake on the east end of the Arboretum.

Audubon
IMPORTANT
BIRD AREAS

Trails

A system of nature trails, over two miles in combined length, weaves through the botanical gardens. The most scenic vistas are along Queen Creek Canyon, with views of Magma Ridge. The Main Trail is about 1½ miles long and passes through the Cactus Garden, past Ayer Lake, near Picketpost Mansion, along Queen Creek and past the Herb Garden before proceeding through the

Eucalyptus Forest. About half of this trail is accessible to wheelchairs, and many side loops from this trail are also accessible.

Site Notes	Fee site. The visitor center features interpretive information and species lists.
Size	1,075 acres (350 acres of gardens and plant collections can be seen with a walk along the main trail)
Directions	Go three miles west of Superior on U.S. Hwy. 60 to milepost #223, or take a 30-minute drive east of Apache Junction on U.S. Hwy. 60.
Nearest Town	Superior
Ownership	Arizona State Parks, Boyce Thompson Arboretum Board, University of Arizona
Contact	520-689-2723 (recorded event/travel info) www.azstateparks.com/Parks/parkhtml/boyce.html ag.arizona.edu/BTA
Facilities	guided tours, workshops, visitor center, interpretive signs, brochure/species list, restrooms, trash cans, trails, overlooks, drinking water, bus/motorhome access, parking, picnic tables and grills

Gila Topminnow

PHOTO BY BRUCE D. TAUBERT

CENTRAL MOUNTAINS ■ Boyce Thompson Arboretum State Park

Premier
★ SITE ★

PHOTO BY CHARLES COBEEN

Gilded Flicker

PHOTO BY BRUCE D. TAUBERT

Description

Nestled amid the red buttes of Papago Park, the Desert Botanical Garden hosts one of the world's finest collections of desert plants. This one-of-a-kind museum showcases acres of beautiful outdoor exhibits. Home to 139 rare, threatened and endangered plant species from around the world, the Garden offers interesting and inspiring experiences to more than 250,000 visitors each year. A surprising number of wildlife species make the garden their home and depending on the time of year, visitors may be treated to any number of resident or visiting "critters."

In 1938 a small group of Valley citizens gathered in Papago Park to create a botanical garden that would encourage an understanding, appreciation, and promotion of the uniqueness of the world's deserts, particularly the Sonoran Desert. The Garden continues to build on its legacy of environmental

CENTRAL MOUNTAINS ■ Desert Botanical Garden

Premier ★ SITE ★

stewardship and has become nationally and internationally renowned for its plant collections, research and educational programs.

The Desert Botanical Garden is home to the world's finest and most diverse collection of succulent plants. Five thematic trails with hands-on activities and interpretive signs welcome visitors. A "Phoenix Point of Pride," it is one of only a few botanical gardens accredited by the American Association of Museums.

Wildlife to Watch

The Desert Botanical Garden is one of the most accessible birding areas in Phoenix where visitors can easily observe many of the more common Sonoran Desert species. Garden plants provide birds with nesting sites and materials, food (seeds, nectar, insects) and places for shelter from predators. Because of the year-round blooming season, nectar is always available and seeds are always ripening.

It would be difficult to find a better location for relaxed viewing and photographing of birds. Gila woodpeckers and gilded flickers excavate holes in the giant saguaros for their nesting cavities. Cholla cacti provide support and spiny protection for the cactus wren's nest. Curve-billed thrashers sing from the tops of the totem pole cactus, while verdins flit around the paloverde trees in search of insects. White-winged doves build nests of twigs on the limbs of trees or on cacti, often near the paths. Gambel's quail spend their days touring the garden looking for food. Many migratory birds and birds of prey visit the garden for short respites or searching for food. You may see multiple varieties of hummingbirds with Anna's, Costa's and black-chinned being the most common. Red-tailed and Harris's hawks are often observed soaring high over the garden. Birders may also find a western screech-owl at the entrance to its saguaro cavity as it warms up in the early morning sun. Many small mammals such as Harris' antelope squirrel, round-tailed ground squirrel, rock squirrel and desert cottontail can be viewed by garden visitors. During warmer months, a variety of lizards and other reptiles frequent the grounds including tiger whiptail, desert spiny lizard, ornate tree lizard, zebra-tailed lizard, gopher snake, coachwhip and common kingsnake.

Docent-led bird walks are held every Monday morning. During the cooler seasons (October through April) the bird walks are held at 8 a.m. During the warmer months (May through September) the bird walks are held at 7 a.m.

Butterflies from around the world can be viewed among beautiful flowering plants in the Butterfly Garden. Check the website below for dates that the Butterfly Garden is open. The Butterfly Garden is highly recommended.

Trails

Five easy trails up to ⅓ mile in length teach about desert life: the Desert Discovery, Plants and People of the Sonoran Desert, Desert Wildflower, Center for Desert Living and Sonoran Desert Nature Trails.

Site Notes	Fee site. There is an additional charge for the Butterfly Garden.
Size	145 acres
Directions	Drive 8 miles east of Central Avenue in Phoenix. From central Phoenix, drive east on McDowell Road, turn right on Galvin Parkway and follow signs. Alternate route: From central Phoenix, drive east on Van Buren Street, turn left on Galvin Parkway and follow signs.
Nearest Town	Phoenix
Ownership	Desert Botanical Garden
Contact	480-941-1225 www.dbg.org/
Facilities	restrooms, trash cans, trails, interpretive signs, drinking water, parking, picnic tables, restaurant, bookstore

Malachite Butterfly   *PHOTO BY CHARLES COBEEN*

Premier
★ SITE ★

Photo by Cindy Marple

American Avocet *PHOTO BY CINDY MARPLE*

Description

In a desert landscape, water is a powerful attractant. This urban nature preserve centers around two areas of desert riparian habitat that attract more than 140 different species of birds and other wildlife.

Consisting of 18 reclaimed water recharge ponds, the riparian preserve was created by the city of Gilbert to provide community wetland wildlife sanctuaries for recreation, education and research. The preserve comprises two separate properties. The Neely Ranch Preserve is not open to the public at present, but the Riparian Preserve at Water Ranch has nearly four miles of walking trails through wildlife habitats that feature burrowing owls and many shorebirds.

At Water Ranch, the Riparian Institute offers education programs for the public, schools and youth groups. Programs range from bird walks to night-viewing programs to dinosaur digs and overnight camps for youth. The permanent lake near the library is open for fishing, with armadas available for picnics and trails for walking, biking and wildlife watching. The preserve also sponsors the annual Feathered Friends Festival in April.

Wildlife to Watch

This is a world-class, year-round bird viewing and photography site. Spring provides one of the region's best opportunities to view breeding activities of

CENTRAL MOUNTAINS ■ Riparian Preserve at Water Ranch

American avocet, black-necked stilt, killdeer, Anna's hummingbird, verdin, Abert's towhee and curve-billed thrasher, to name a few. In the late summer when the desert broom plant is blooming, hundreds of butterflies are attracted to its sweet nectar. During the winter, hundreds of waterfowl and waterbirds are attracted to these shallow open ponds, such as ring-necked duck, redhead, lesser scaup, cinnamon and green-winged teals, mallard, northern pintail, gadwall, bufflehead, northern shoveler, great and snowy egrets, great blue and green herons, and black-crowned night-herons. On most winter and spring days, osprey can be seen fishing on the large pond. Other birds of prey include peregrine falcon, American kestrel and red-tailed hawk. Although still fairly new, the preserve has already attracted several species that are quite rare in Arizona, including streak-backed oriole, groove-billed ani and prairie warbler.

Audubon
IMPORTANT
BIRD AREAS

Trails

4½ miles of universally accessible trails.

Size	175 acres (Neely Ranch 72 acres; Riparian Preserve at Water Ranch 110 acres)
Directions	The preserve is located 21 miles southeast of Phoenix. Take U.S. 60 to the Greenfield Road exit, drive south 1½ miles to Guadalupe Road and either turn left and enter off Guadalupe Road or drive through the intersection and turn left into site from Greenfield Road.
Nearest Town	Gilbert
Ownership	city of Gilbert/The Riparian Institute
Contact	480-503-6744 www.riparianinstitute.org/
Facilities	restrooms, trash cans, trails, interpretive signs, drinking water, parking, picnic tables, children's playground, photo blinds, ramadas

CENTRAL MOUNTAINS ■ *Riparian Preserve at Water Ranch*

Premier
★ SITE ★

Verdin

PHOTO BY BRUCE D. TAUBERT

Green-winged Teal

PHOTO BY CINDY MARPLE

Premier
★ SITE ★

Dead Horse Ranch State Park

Verde River Greenway State Natural Area

Dead Horse Ranch State Park

PHOTO BY GEORGE ANDREJKO

Description

Walk along a rare free-flowing desert river, listen to the whisper of cottonwood leaves in a gentle breeze and look for birds. At the heart of this park, located at about 3,300 feet elevation, runs the Verde River. A dense forest of riparian trees and shrubs line the Verde's banks. Part of a designated Important Bird Area, this Fremont cottonwood/Gooding willow riparian gallery forest is one of only five stands remaining in Arizona and one of 20 such stands in the world.

Three lagoons at the park provide opportunities for fishing and wildlife viewing. The park is also ideal for camping, hiking, canoeing, picnicking, fishing or mountain biking in the adjacent Coconino National Forest.

Wildlife to Watch

A six-mile reach of the river known as the Verde River Greenway State Natural Area supports a diversity of unique species, including bald eagle, willow flycatcher, terrestrial gartersnake, gopher snake, plateau lizard and lowland leopard frog. You may also see common black-hawk, osprey, yellow-billed cuckoo, Gambel's quail and numerous migratory bird species. Mammals include beaver, raccoon, ringtail, mule deer, javelina, bobcat and coyote. This is one of the few places in Arizona where you have a chance to see river otter.

Audubon
IMPORTANT
BIRD AREAS

CENTRAL MOUNTAINS ■ *Dead Horse Ranch State Park*

Great
▲ SITE ▲

Trails

A well-developed and well-marked trail system exists in the park, with trails ranging from ¼ miles to the 15-mile historic Lime Kiln Trail that connects Dead Horse State Park to Red Rock State Park. Some trails are multi-use, with mountain biking and equestrian use. Some trails feature interpretive signage and universal accessibility.

Site Notes	The Verde Valley Birding and Nature Festival is held each April; Verde River Days is celebrated in September.
Size	920 acres
Directions	From Cottonwood, take Main Street and turn north on North 10th Street. Cross the Verde River Bridge to the park entrance.
Nearest Town	Cottonwood
Ownership	Arizona State Parks
Contact	928-634-5283 www.azstateparks.com/Parks/parkhtml/deadhorse.html
Facilities	accessible restrooms, accessible trails, accessible campground, accessible cabins, hiking trails with river access, stocked fishing lagoons, motorhome facilities, lookouts, brochure/bird species list, visitor center, drinking water, parking, trash cans

Lowland Leopard Frog

PHOTO BY THOMAS C. BRENNAN

Great
▲ SITE ▲

CENTRAL MOUNTAINS ■ *Montezuma Castle National Monument*

Montezuma Castle National Monument

PHOTO BY GEORGE ANDREJKO

Description

One of the best-preserved cliff dwellings in North America attracts visitors to this national monument in the Verde Valley of central Arizona. Located at a junction between the Colorado Plateau and the Basin and Range regions, the five-story, 20-room cliff-dwelling was home to the Sinagua people in about 1200 A.D.

The dwelling, known as Montezuma Castle, overlooks Beaver Creek. Sycamore riparian habitat along this creek provides rich habitat for birds and other wildlife. The monument also includes Montezuma Well, a unique habitat formed when an immense cavern collapsed to form a limestone sink. This sink has a flow of more than one-half million gallons of water per day.

Wildlife to Watch

Nocturnal animals include woodrat, pocket gopher, skunk, ringtail, a variety of bats, amphibians, such as Woodhouse's and red-spotted toads and owls. Animals that are most active at dawn and dusk include mule deer, coyote, porcupine, desert cottontail, black-tailed jackrabbit and many songbirds. A few desert animals are primarily active during the day, including hawks and eagles, Clark's and desert spiny lizards and black-necked and terrestrial gartersnakes.

During the spring and summer breeding seasons, black-throated sparrow, Bewick's wren and brown-headed cowbird are among the most common species, although frequently observed riparian birds include Cooper's hawk, common black-hawk, belted kingfisher, Gila and ladder-backed woodpeckers,

Great
▲ SITE ▲

black phoebe, Bell's vireo, bridled and juniper titmouse, Lucy's and yellow warblers, summer tanager and hooded, Bullock's and Scott's orioles.

Trails

A ⅓-mile loop trail is located at Montezuma Well. At the cliff dwellings, a ⅓-mile trail provides interpretive signage about cultural and natural history.

Site Notes	Early morning and off-season visitation may be more productive for wildlife viewing.
Size	920 acres
Directions	To reach Montezuma Well, take exit 293 from I-17 and drive 4 miles. To reach Montezuma Castle and Sinagua Indian cliff dwellings take exit 289 and go ½ mile past Cliff Castle Casino to reach the access road. The site is 3 miles from I-17.
Nearest Town	Camp Verde
Ownership	National Park Service
Contact	928-567-5276 www.nps.gov/moca/
Facilities	restrooms, trash cans, trails, interpretive signs, visitor center, drinking water, parking

Ringtail

PHOTO BY GEORGE ANDREJKO

Great
▲ SITE ▲

Page Springs Hatchery/Bubbling Ponds Hatchery and Wildlife Viewing Trail

Riparian birds in a gallery of cottonwood trees; operational fish hatchery

CENTRAL MOUNTAINS ■ Page Springs Hatchery/Bubbling Ponds Hatchery and Wildlife Viewing Trail

Page Springs Hatchery/Bubbling Ponds Hatchery & Wildlife Viewing Trail PHOTO BY BRUCE D. TAUBERT

Description

Located between Sedona and Cottonwood along scenic Oak Creek, two fish hatcheries attract wildlife year-round.

The Page Springs Hatchery is the state's largest trout-growing facility, while nearby Bubbling Ponds Hatchery raises warmwater fish species such as largemouth bass, smallmouth bass and bluegill. Native species include Colorado River pikeminnow and razorback sucker.

Both hatcheries offer wildlife-viewing areas, parking and trails. The trails at Page Springs are more developed than those at Bubbling Ponds. Page Springs features a visitor center with interpretive exhibits on trout production and area wildlife. The Bubbling Ponds viewing trail enters a huge cottonwood gallery and mesquite bosque.

Wildlife to Watch

During the winter, the ponds at Bubbling Ponds offer great viewing opportunities for migratory waterfowl, including ring-necked and ruddy ducks, common goldeneye, mallard, northern pintail, northern shoveler, cinnamon and green-winged teals. Wood duck, common merganser, common black-hawk and belted kingfisher often nest along Oak Creek. When ponds are low, the careful observer may spot Wilson's snipe among the emergent vegetation at the water's edge. During the warmer months, rufous, black-chinned, broad-tailed, Anna's and Costa's hummingbirds are common. Egrets and herons are always present looking for an easy meal. Mule deer and

Great
▲ SITE ▲

javelina are often seen on the Bubbling Ponds trail. Birds include summer tanager, Lucy's and yellow warblers, hooded and Bullock's orioles, and brown-crested flycatcher. This is one of the few places in Arizona where you have a chance to see river otter. The entire family will enjoy the opportunity to view and feed the large rainbow trout at the show pond. Visitors may encounter a variety of reptiles and amphibians in the area. The lucky visitor may catch a glimpse of the Mexican or narrow-headed gartersnakes as they slide through the reeds and rushes at the water's edge.

Audubon
IMPORTANT
BIRD AREAS

Trails

1½ miles of smoothed trails loop the two sites. The trailhead and parking lot is open 365 days a year from sunrise to sunset.

Site Notes	Self-guided trails and tours of hatchery facilities are available. There is an interpretive visitor center at Page Springs. Hatchery hours are from 8 a.m. to 4 p.m. every day of the year except Thanksgiving and Christmas.
Size	220 acres (Page Springs 83 acres, Bubbling Ponds 137 acres)
Directions	The site is located 10 miles south of Sedona and 10 miles north of Cottonwood off Hwy. 89A on the Page Springs Road. Access is also available from I-17 via the McGuireville Exit (exit 293). West 10 miles to Cornville, turn north on Page Springs Road for 5½ miles.
Nearest Town	Sedona/Cottonwood
Ownership	Arizona Game and Fish Department
Contact	928-634-4466 www.azgfd.gov/h_f/hatcheries_page_springs.shtml
Facilities	accessible restrooms and trails, overlooks, interpretive signs, brochure, bird species list, visitor center, bus/motorhome access, parking

Common Black-hawk   PHOTO BY BRIAN E. SMALL

Great
▲ SITE ▲

CENTRAL MOUNTAINS ■ *Page Springs Hatchery/Bubbling Ponds Hatchery and Wildlife Viewing Trail*

Red Rock State Park

PHOTO BY ARIZONA STATE PARKS

Description

Spectacular red rock cliffs frame this 286-acre nature preserve and environmental center on Oak Creek. Riparian tree species such as Fremont cottonwood, Goodding's willow, Bonpland willow, Arizona walnut, Arizona sycamore, western soapberry and velvet ash thrive here, attracting rare and unique birds.

Oak Creek is designated as a "Unique Water of Arizona." The park, located at 3,800 to 4,200 feet elevation, is part of an Important Bird Area designated by the Audubon Society and a fine place to learn about birds. In addition to lush riparian habitat, Red Rock State Park offers chaparral and pinyon-juniper woodland. The blend of habitats makes this an important migratory stopover site for many kinds of songbirds.

Wildlife to Watch

Over 172 species of birds have been identified. During the warmer months, expect to see Anna's, black-chinned and broad-tailed hummingbirds at the feeders located at the visitor center. Rarely, you might see a magnificent hummingbird, and during the migration season, rufous hummingbirds frequent the feeders. Birds of prey include eight species of hawks, eagles and falcons, including zone-tailed hawk, bald eagle and peregrine falcon. Breeding bird species of special interest include the wood duck, common merganser, yellow-billed cuckoo and common black-hawk.

Mammal species include the mule deer, javelina, river otter, ringtail, striped skunk and Arizona gray squirrel. Reptiles and amphibians include gopher snake,

CENTRAL MOUNTAINS ▪ Red Rock State Park

Great
▲ SITE ▲

ring-necked snake, terrestrial gartersnake, western patch-nosed snake, striped and Sonoran whipsnakes, common kingsnake, black-tailed, western diamond-backed and Arizona black rattlesnakes, greater short-horned, plateau, ornate tree and Madrean alligator lizards, plateau striped whiptail, canyon treefrog, Woodhouse's toad and Sonoran mud turtle. This is also an excellent place to view butterflies, damselflies, dragonflies and other interesting invertebrates.

Audubon
IMPORTANT
BIRD AREAS

Trails

A 5-mile network of interconnecting loops lead to vistas of red rock or along the lush greenery of Oak Creek. Three major loops are the Eagle's Nest, Apache Fire and Coyote Ridge Trails. The Kisva Trail connects these and leads up to the short loop of the Yavapai Ridge Trail. The Javelina Trail goes into the pinyon-juniper woodlands; Rattlesnake Ridge rises above a picnic area; and the Smoke Trail runs along Oak Creek. All trails start from the visitor center.

Site Notes	Many educational and interpretive programs are provided at the visitor center and throughout the park, including guided hikes, bird walks and moonlight hikes.
Size	286 acres
Directions	From Sedona, take 89A south for 5⅓ miles. Turn left onto Lower Red Rock Loop Road for approximately 2½ miles.
Nearest Town	Sedona
Ownership	Arizona State Parks
Contact	928-282-6907 www.azstateparks.com/Parks/parkhtml/redrock.html
Facilities	accessible restrooms and trails, overlooks, interpretive signs, brochure, bird species list, visitor center, bus/motorhome access, parking

Zone-tailed Hawk   PHOTO BY BRIAN E. SMALL

Great
▲ SITE ▲

Roosevelt Lake Wildlife Area

PHOTO BY GEORGE ANDREJKO

Description

Set in the lush upper Sonoran Desert, Roosevelt Lake is 23 miles long, with about 128 miles of shoreline and a surface area of about 21,000 acres (depending on rainfall). Two major drainages—Salt River and Tonto Creek—feed into the lake.

The wildlife area at the west end of Roosevelt Lake is surrounded by Four Peaks, Superstition, Mazatzal and Sierra Ancha mountain ranges, making it a picturesque place to view desert wildlife. Habitats here consist of upper Sonoran Desert, marsh, open water and (depending on flows) inundated vegetation. Visitors can expect sweltering summer temperatures, while winter temperatures may drop below freezing.

Wildlife to Watch

Roosevelt Lake and the wildlife area are the winter home for a large flock of Canada geese. Hundreds of wild geese can sometimes be seen in the Bermuda Flat area, where they graze on grass and forbs. The water also attracts snow geese and a great variety of other waterfowl and grebes during migration and winter. Large numbers of western grebes and fewer numbers of Clark's grebes have recently become permanent residents on the lake.

Herons, cormorants, willow flycatcher, bald eagle and osprey are just a few of the numerous species that live and nest in the wildlife area. A well-developed cottonwood-willow riparian forest borders Tonto Creek just before it enters the lake near the A Cross Road. Look in this area for yellow-billed cuckoo, hooded oriole, summer tanager and other highly sought-after riparian species.

CENTRAL MOUNTAINS ■ Roosevelt Lake Wildlife Area

Great
▲ SITE ▲

Deer, javelina, coyote, ringtail and numerous varieties of ground squirrels, snakes and lizards inhabit the area. Near the wetlands visitors may encounter a variety of amphibians and reptiles, including common kingsnake, black-necked garter-snake, Sonoran mud turtle, Woodhouse's toad, and desert spiny and ornate tree lizards. The uplands are home to western diamond-backed rattlesnake, and eastern collared, common side-blotched and greater earless lizards.

Trails

Several trailheads lead into the surrounding mountain ranges.

Site Notes	Part of the wildlife area is a wildlife refuge. During the time that Canada geese are present a portion is closed to public entry and during the hunting season a portion is closed to hunting. View geese and other waterfowl in winter along the lakeshore from State Hwy. 188.
Size	286 acres
Directions	From Mesa, take Hwy. 87 north for about 60 miles to the junction of Hwy. 87 and Hwy. 188. Turn right and follow Hwy. 188 south for 26 miles to the lake. From the Tucson area take Hwy. 77 to Globe, then Hwy. 60 south, then Hwy. 188 north for 27 miles to the lake.
Nearest Town	Roosevelt or Tonto Basin
Ownership	U.S.D.A. Forest Service, Tonto National Forest
Contact	928-467-3200 www.fs.fed.us/outdoors/naturewatch/arizona/wildlife/roosevelt-lake/index.shtml
Facilities	restrooms, trash cans, trails, lookouts, interpretive signs, brochure/species list, visitor center, drinking water, bus/motorhome access, boat ramps, parking

Javelina   *PHOTO BY PAUL BERQUIST*

Great
▲ SITE ▲

South Mountain Park

PHOTO BY BRUCE D. TAUBERT

Description

South Mountain Park, at nearly 17,000 acres, is the nation's largest municipal park. The rugged desert mountain terrain, with easy access from Phoenix, provides scenic mountain vistas. The park also offers an environmental education center, guided programs, several picnic areas and an extensive trail system. Spring wildflower displays can be spectacular following adequate winter rains. Attractions include night wildlife-watching and scorpion searches; the site also includes excellent views of the city lights.

Wildlife to Watch

Red-tailed and Harris's hawks, javelina, coyote, gray fox, white-throated woodrat, pocket mouse and ringtail have all been recorded in this park. Common Sonoran Desert birds such as Costa's hummingbird, cactus and rock wrens, black-tailed gnatcatcher, curve-billed thrasher, Gambel's quail, greater roadrunner and verdin are found here. The pavilion and picnic area near the environmental education center is one of the more reliable locations to observe resident Bendire's thrasher in the Phoenix area. Birders may also find canyon wren, canyon towhee, rufous-crowned sparrow and Scott's oriole (best in early spring) along pull-outs near the end of the drive to the top of the mountain. A unique orange-tailed common chuckwalla is one of the largest and easily observed of the park's lizards. They favor boulder-strewn hillsides where they can be seen basking on warm spring mornings. Other reptiles include tiger whiptail, gopher snake, speckled and western diamond-backed rattlesnakes.

Great
▲ SITE ▲

Trails

18 different trails range in length from 1 to 14 miles. All have steep, rugged and rocky sections. Check at the entrance for trail maps and accessibility.

Site Notes Fee site. Six species of rattlesnakes can be found in and around South Mountain. Warm weather visitors should take appropriate precautions when hiking or recreating in the park and adjacent areas to avoid snakes. Though snake encounters are not uncommon, bites from these animals are rare.

Size 16,000 acres

Directions From I-10, take Baseline Rd. west to Central Avenue, and Central Ave. south to the park.

Nearest Town Phoenix

Ownership city of Phoenix

Contact 602-495-5811
phoenix.gov/PARKS/hikesoth.html

Features restrooms, trash cans, trails, lookouts, interpretive signs, visitor center, drinking water, bus/motorhome access, parking, picnic areas

Common Chuckwalla   PHOTO BY WILLIAM WELLS

Great
▲ SITE ▲

Tavasci Marsh/Tuzigoot National Monument   *PHOTO BY GEORGE ANDREJKO*

Description

Tavasci Marsh formed thousands of years ago in a now-abandoned meander of the Verde River. It provides wetland habitat for a great diversity of plant and animal life in the Verde River valley.

The marsh was undoubtedly important in supporting the ancient Sinagua pueblo located just uphill, now protected in Tuzigoot National Monument. The Sinagua were agriculturalists with trade connections that extended for hundreds of miles. Their pueblo, which was inhabited from around 1000 A.D. to around 1400 A.D., consisted of 110 rooms, including two- and three-story structures. Its ruins are a fascinating record of this ancient people.

Wildlife to Watch

A variety of water birds including wood duck, great blue heron, least bittern, sora, Virginia rail, common yellowthroat and red-winged blackbird can be seen at the marsh. Yellow warbler, brown-crested flycatcher, yellow-billed cuckoo and summer tanager utilize riparian vegetation. Birds of prey include red-tailed and Cooper's hawks, common black-hawk and great horned owl. Mammals include mule deer, coyote, ringtail, striped skunk and a variety of bats. Woodhouse's toad and lowland leopard frog along with terrestrial gartersnake are a few of the amphibian and reptile species that live there.

Audubon
IMPORTANT
BIRD AREAS

CENTRAL MOUNTAINS ■ *Tavasci Marsh/Tuzigoot National Monument*

Great
▲ SITE ▲

Trails

The Visitor Center and Tavasci Marsh Overlook trails at Tuzigoot are universally accessible. The Ruins Loop Trail is ¼ mile. There are no formal trails at Tavasci Marsh.

Site Notes — Viewing and interpretation at Tuzigoot focus on the pueblo and an overlook trail to Tavasci Marsh, with scenic vistas of the marsh, Verde River, Verde Valley and Mingus Mountain. The Visitor Center offers guided tours and interpretive displays.

Size — 136 acres (marsh); 58 acres (monument)

Directions — Take I-17 to exit 287 and then Hwy. 260 to Cottonwood. In Cottonwood, take Main Street toward Clarkdale and look for highway signs to marsh and monument.

Nearest Town — Cottonwood/Clarkdale

Ownership — Arizona Game and Fish Department/National Park Service

Contact — 928-774-5045 (AGFD), 928-634-5564 (NPS)
www.nps.gov/tuzi/

Features — restrooms, trash cans, trails, lookouts, interpretive signs, brochure/species list, visitor center, drinking water, bus/motorhome access, parking

Summer Tanager

PHOTO BY BRIAN E. SMALL

Great
▲ SITE ▲

Canyon Creek and Canyon Creek Hatchery

30

Description

Canyon Creek, an outstanding high elevation riparian community of 840 acres just under the Mogollon Rim, is a very popular fishing and birding destination. Canyon Creek Hatchery is built at the headwaters that feed into Canyon Creek. In 2000, a large wildfire swept through the area surrounding the hatchery. After the fire, elk, deer and other wildlife species moved into the area to take advantage of the lush growth that resulted from the burn.

Wildlife to Watch

Canyon Creek is an excellent place to view elk, mule deer, Merriam's turkey, Abert's squirrel and trout year round. It is also a great spot to view waterfowl and a wide range of riparian birds, especially during the spring migration. You may see black-chinned, broad-tailed and rufous hummingbirds, Mexican spotted owl, belted kingfisher and American dipper. The cottonwood and willow stands along the drainage attract many nesting birds including common black-hawk, zone-tailed hawk, Cassin's kingbird and Brewer's blackbird. In winter and spring, bald eagle forage at the hatchery show pond. Canyon Creek is home to rainbow and brown trout and many of the small fish that can be seen from the shore are speckled dace, one of Arizona's native fish species.

Trails

There are no official trails but you can view wildlife by walking the forested area along the creek. There is a self-guided tour of the hatchery work areas; hiking routes at the hatchery are paved but grades are steep.

Site Notes The access road is a winding dirt road that can be closed during wet or snowy conditions. This road is best traveled with high clearance vehicles.

Directions The hatchery is located 45 miles east of Payson on Hwy. 260. Turn south on Young Road (Forest Road 512) and continue for approximately 3 miles. Turn east on FR 33 (under the power lines) and continue 5 miles to the hatchery in upper Canyon Creek.

Contact Arizona Game and Fish Department; 928-535-5475 (radio phone); www.azgfd.govs/h_f/hatcheries_canyon_creek.shtml

Features restrooms, interpretive center, drinking water, parking, bus/motorhome access

Crescent Moon Picnic Area

Description

One of the most photographed scenes in the Southwest is towering Cathedral Rock reflected in the waters of Oak Creek at Red Rock Crossing. The picnic area located at that same site is as popular as it is beautiful. At times it can be quite crowded, but if you come early in the morning or on a weekday, it is possible to have the world class beauty of Red Rock Crossing nearly to yourself.

Wildlife to Watch

Excellent birding along the creek area includes springtime migratory birds such as Bullock's oriole, black-throated gray warbler, western and Cassin's kingbirds, common black-hawk and black-chinned hummingbird. Resident birds include great blue heron, American kestrel, Cooper's hawk, great horned owl, Gambel's quail, belted kingfisher and western scrub-jay. Other wildlife includes javelina, mule deer, raccoon, rock squirrel, terrestrial gartersnake, ring-necked snake, plateau lizard, ornate tree lizard and collared lizard.

Trails

Paved walkways access the riparian area, Oak Creek, the historic waterwheel and interpretive kiosks.

Directions Drive west from Sedona on U.S. 89A. Just outside town, turn south on FR 216 (Upper Red Rock Loop Road). Drive about 1½ miles and follow the signs to Red Rock Crossing.

Contact U.S.D.A. Forest Service, Coconino National Forest; 928-204-1398; www.fs.fed.us/r3/coconino/recreation/red_rock/crescentmoon-picnic.shtml

Features restrooms, trash cans, trails, interpretive signs, brochure/species list, drinking water, bus/motorhome access, parking

Goldwater Lake Park   32

Description

An easy scenic drive through the mountains just outside Prescott leads to this clear, clean lake surrounded by tall ponderosa pine forest.

Wildlife to Watch

The main draw here is birding: the lake attracts great blue heron, American coot, double-crested cormorant and many ducks such as common merganser, ring-necked duck and mallard. Look for bald eagle, osprey and various species of woodpeckers including northern flicker, hairy and acorn woodpeckers. Other species that may be observed throughout the year are Steller's jay, mountain chickadee, white-breasted and pygmy nuthatches, brown creeper, dark-eyed junco and during good pine cone crop years, red crossbill. Spring and summer months bring many migratory species to breed among the pines.

Trails

A trail surrounding the lake begins in the parking lot. The trail exits the park into the Prescott National Forest after about a mile.

Directions Go 4 miles south of Prescott on Senator Highway. Mt. Vernon Street in the Historic Downtown area becomes Senator Highway outside the city limits. Take South Mt. Vernon St. out of town to the park entrance.

Contact city of Prescott; 928-777-1564; www.cityofprescott.net/services/parks/parks.php

Features restrooms, trash cans, trails, drinking water, bus/motorhome access, boat ramps, parking, trail

Other sites

Heritage Park/Willow Lake

Description

Views of the mountains surrounding Prescott and the unique rock formations of the Granite Dells make this a striking, picturesque place. The 647-acre park is an Important Bird Area. The Willow Lake Archaeological Interpretive Center features three excavated pithouses, circa 850–1100 A.D.

Wildlife to Watch

Over 20 species of waterfowl have been observed. Great blue heron and double-crested cormorant nest in the cottonwood stand along Willow Lake. Depending on water levels, many species of shorebirds, gulls and terns can be found during spring and fall migration. Bald eagle and osprey are occasionally observed at the lake. There is interpretive signage and a wildlife viewing station.

Audubon
IMPORTANT
BIRD AREAS

Trails

3½ miles of trail partially circles Willow Lake with access points from within Heritage Park and from the back of Willow Creek Park.

Directions From four miles north of Prescott on Willow Lake Road, turn onto Heritage Park Road across from the entrance to Embry Riddle Aeronautical University. Turn right into Heritage Park and proceed past the zoo entrance into Heritage Park.

Contact city of Prescott; 928-777-1564; www.cityofprescott.net/services/parks/parks.php

Features restrooms, trash cans, trails, lookouts, interpretive signs, drinking water, bus/motorhome access, boat ramps, parking

Lake Pleasant Regional Park

Description

One of the most scenic water recreation areas in the "Valley of the Sun," this northwest Valley park offers many activities, including wildlife viewing. Nestled in beautiful paloverde and saguaro-studded desert, this 24,000-acre site is just a short drive north from the Phoenix metropolitan area.

Wildlife to Watch

Deer, javelina, coyote, fox, gray squirrel, Harris' antelope squirrel and multiple bird species including peregrine falcon and nesting bald eagles in the winter and spring are main wildlife attractions. Flocks of American white pelicans and the occasional brown pelican (late summer) stop by the lake during migration. In addition, multiple reptiles inhabit the area, including desert tortoise, desert spiny lizard, zebra-tailed lizard, coachwhip, common kingsnake, and speckled and western diamond-backed rattlesnakes.

Other sites

Trails

Lake Pleasant Regional Park offers over four miles of trails, ranging in length from ½ mile to 2 miles, and easy to moderate in difficulty. The Pipeline Canyon Trail includes a floating bridge for use during high water levels. The Visitor Center Trail is an easy ½ mile. The Roadrunner Trail is a scenic 1½-mile trail.

Directions Located thirty minutes north of Phoenix (near Peoria), this site can be reached from the south or north via I-17 to Hwy. 74, then west approximately 10 miles to Castle Hot Springs Road.

Contact Maricopa County Parks; 602-372-7460; www.maricopa.gov/parks/lake_pleasant

Features restrooms, trash cans, trails, overlooks, interpretive signs, brochure/bird species list, visitor center, drinking water, bus/motorhome access, boat ramps, parking

Lost Dutchman State Park · 35

Description

Located in the Sonoran Desert foothills, this 320-acre park provides a scenic view of the famous Superstition Mountains, site of the legendary Lost Dutchman gold mine. At 2,000 feet elevation, the desert is lush with paloverde, ironwood trees and giant saguaro cactus. Desert wildflowers can be spectacular after winter rains.

Wildlife to Watch

Common birds are Costa's hummingbird, gilded flicker, Gila and ladder-backed woodpeckers, cactus and rock wrens, phainopepla, verdin, black-tailed gnatcatcher, Gambel's quail, curve-billed thrasher, and Harris's and red-tailed hawks. Mule deer, javelina, gray fox, ringtail and even mountain lion can be found in the area.

Trails

Six trails range in length from ½ mile to 4 miles: Treasure Loop, Prospector's View, Jacob's Crosscut, Siphon Draw, Discovery and Native Plant Trails. The Discovery and Native Plant Trails feature interpretive signage.

Directions From Apache Junction, go northeast on the Apache Trail (AZ 88) for 5 miles to the park entrance.

Contact Arizona State Parks; 480-982-4485 www.azstateparks.com/Parks/parkhtml/dutchman.html

Features restrooms, trash cans, trails, interpretive signs, brochure/species list, visitor center, drinking water, bus/motorhome access, parking, campground, picnic area

Other sites

Lower Salt River

Description

A scenic lake, a riparian area along Lynx Creek, and a variety of habitat types in a relatively small space combine to make this 200-acre recreation area an excellent place to watch birds and other wildlife. Visitors enjoy the Lynx Creek Gold Pan area, the Lynx Creek Ruin Trail and the North Shore Scenic Vista Overlook. The Highlands Center for Natural History offers outdoor science education.

Wildlife to Watch

Wildlife can best be viewed along the river. Bald eagle, osprey, peregrine falcon, Harris's hawk, herons, egrets, waterfowl, and other riparian and upland birds are frequently observed. Many species of migratory songbirds also appear during the spring to nest in the area, such as black-chinned and Costa's hummingbirds, vermilion and ash-throated flycatchers, Bell's vireo, Lucy's warbler and hooded oriole. Beaver are occasionally seen along the riverbank or swimming in the water. Of the various lizards, snakes and toads found in the area, the gopher snake, coachwhip, western diamond-backed rattlesnake, desert spiny and zebra-tailed lizards and Woodhouse's toad are most common.

Audubon
IMPORTANT
BIRD AREAS

Site Notes Fee site. Vehicle and foot traffic prohibited from December 1 to June 30 along the south side of the Salt River near Water Users Recreation Area to protect nesting bald eagles. The Blue Point and Sheep's Crossing recreation areas may also be closed December to June to protect nesting bald eagles downstream.

Directions From Mesa or U.S. 60 take either Power Road or Ellsworth (Usery Pass) Road north to the Bush Highway, which extends along the Lower Salt River. Access. Paved parking is available at the Granite Reef, Phon D. Sutton, Coon Bluff, Goldfield, Blue Point and Water Users sites.

Contact U.S.D.A. Forest Service, Tonto National Forest; 480-610-3300

Features restrooms, trash cans, bus/motorhome access, picnic tables, paved parking, riverside access

Lynx Lake Recreation Area

37

Description

This 200-acre recreation area combines a scenic lake, a riparian area along Lynx Creek and a variety of habitat types in a relatively small area. Areas include the Lynx Creek Gold Pan area, the Lynx Creek Ruin Trail and the North Shore Scenic Vista overlook. The Highlands Center for Natural History offers outdoor science education.

Other sites

Wildlife to Watch

From the North Shore Vista Point, visitors have a wonderful view of the lake including bald eagle roosts and a nest site. The lake attracts mule deer, javelina, great blue heron, osprey, great horned owl, belted kingfisher and double-crested cormorant. The ponderosa pine, scrub oak and pinyon-juniper woodlands surrounding the lake hold a wide variety of resident and breeding bird species. Many reptiles also inhabit the area including plateau lizard, greater short-horned lizard, Sonoran whipsnake, gopher snake and Arizona black rattlesnake.

Trails

The main trail, a 2⅓-mile loop around Lynx Lake, is open year-round and provides universal accessibility. This location is the best place for viewing bald eagles and waterfowl at the site.

Directions From Prescott, go east on State Hwy. 69 for 4 miles to Walker Road. Turn south (right) and proceed for 3 miles to the Lynx Lake Recreation Area.

Contact U.S.D.A. Forest Service, Prescott National Forest; 928-443-8000; www.fs.fed.us/r3/prescott/fishing/fishing_lynx.htm

Features restrooms, trash cans, trails, lookouts, interpretive signs, brochure/bird species list, drinking water, bus/motorhome access, boat ramps, parking, campsites, picnic tables

Tonto Creek Hatchery   38

Description

Located in a marvelous canyon, Tonto Creek Hatchery is the most-visited of the state's five fish hatcheries. Its riparian habitat along Tonto Creek is an excellent site to view wildlife, including elk.

Wildlife to Watch

A wide range of riparian birds can be seen, including great blue heron, belted kingfisher and osprey. American dipper can also be found, particularly during the fall and winter. Riparian breeding birds along the creek include common black-hawk, broad-tailed hummingbird, bridled titmouse, Virginia's and MacGillivray's warblers, black-headed grosbeak and occasionally indigo bunting. Merriam's turkey, band-tailed pigeon, acorn woodpecker, nuthatches and towhees also frequent the area. Reptiles and amphibians include Mexican gartersnake, Sonoran mountain kingsnake, Arizona black rattlesnake, greater short-horned lizard, plateau lizard, many-lined skink, Arizona treefrog and Arizona toad. The hatchery raises Arizona's state fish, the Apache trout, as well as rainbow and brown trout.

Trails

Hatchery work areas are paved for self-guided tours. The famed Highline Trail can be accessed near the parking lot.

Directions Drive 21 miles east of Payson off Hwy. 260. Turn north at signed road near Kohl's Ranch and travel 4 miles to end of road.

Other sites

Contact Arizona Game and Fish Department; 928-478-4200
www.azgfd.gov/h_f/hatcheries_tonto_creek.shtml

Features accessible restroom, interpretive center, drinking water, parking,
bus/motorhome access, trash cans

Tonto Creek Recreation Area 39

Description

Protected beneath the Mogollon Rim, this five-acre recreation area is
particularly popular in summer. Cottonwood, willow, Arizona walnut,
sycamore and Rocky Mountain maple comprise the canyon habitat. In
1990, the Dude Fire burned 24,000 acres nearby; self-guided auto tours
show fire damage and recovery.

Wildlife to Watch

A wide variety of song and other birds are here, including Merriam's turkey,
band-tailed pigeon, American dipper, Virginia's and MacGillivray's warblers
and acorn woodpecker. Rufous, black-chinned and broad-tailed hummingbirds are common in spring and summer. Mammals include elk, mule deer,
Abert's squirrel, Arizona gray squirrel and rock squirrel. A variety of reptiles
and amphibians may be encountered along the creek and its canyon.

Trails

Several trails with easy access to wildlife viewing.

Directions From Payson, go east on Hwy. 260 for 17 miles to Tonto Creek
Recreation Area, north on Forest Road 289.

Contact U.S.D.A. Forest Service, Tonto National Forest; 928-474-7900
www.fs.fed.us/outdoors/naturewatch/arizona/wildlife/
tonto-creek/index.shtml

Features restrooms, trash cans, trails, interpretive signs, bus/motorhome
access, parking

Tonto Natural Bridge State Park 40

Description

Tucked away in a tiny valley surrounded by a forest of ponderosa pine trees,
Tonto Natural Bridge is believed to be the largest natural travertine bridge in
the world. Two waterfalls cascading from the top of the arch create an
unusually moist habitat for wildlife.

Wildlife to Watch

Birds include American dipper, canyon wren, Bell's vireo, downy and acorn
woodpeckers, ash-throated flycatcher, band-tailed pigeon, bridled titmouse,
phainopepla and black-headed grosbeak. The canyon is also home to rock
squirrel, raccoon and the nocturnal ringtail.

Other sites

Trails

Three trails lead through the canyon to the natural bridge. All are steep and difficult; the Pine Creek Trail is ½ mile long, steep and undeveloped. The Waterfall Trail is 300 feet long, developed but with uneven steps; and the Gowan Loop Trail is ½ mile long, steep and rough.

Directions This site is located off State Hwy. 87, about 10 miles northwest of Payson. The road into the park is paved, but steep and narrow.

Contact Arizona State Parks; 928-476-4202
www.azstateparks.com/Parks/parkhtml/tonto.html

Features visitor center, trails, overlooks, picnic tables, cabins

Tres Rios Wetlands   41

Description

Tres Rios is a 35-acre wetland complex constructed for wastewater treatment at the confluence of the Salt, Gila and Agua Fria rivers. A premier birding area close to metropolitan Phoenix, the created habitats shelter many species of waterfowl in winter. Although not well-developed, this site offers excellent viewing opportunities to the knowledgeable birder.

Wildlife to Watch

More than 150 different species of birds have been spotted in the area. You may see three species of egrets, green and great blue herons, black-crowned night-herons, white-faced ibis, neotropic cormorant, yellow-headed and red-winged blackbirds, least bittern, black-bellied whistling-duck and black-necked stilt. The cottonwood trees and shrubs attract many migratory and wintering songbirds. During late fall and early winter, these trees are frequently full of foraging yellow-rumped and orange-crowned warblers, and less common species such as black-throated gray, Townsend's, yellow, and black-and-white warblers. The site also contains a great blue heron rookery near the parking area.

Audubon
IMPORTANT
BIRD AREAS

Trails

A trail runs along the creek among cottonwoods, mesquite and willows and accesses all three ponds; portions of the trail have universal accessibility.

Directions Located 13 miles southwest of central Phoenix. Go west on I-10 (Papago Freeway) to the 91st Ave exit, then south for 4⅗ mi to the Main Gate of the Waste Water Treatment Plant on left. Go ¼ mi on 91st Ave to Gate 3 and drive straight back to fenced parking.

Contact city of Phoenix; 602-495-7927; phoenix.gov/TRESRIOS/index.html

Features trails, interpretive signs, parking, picnic area

CENTRAL MOUNTAINS ■ Other Sites

Upper Verde River Wildlife Area 42

Description

Several of the source springs for the Verde River originate on this 796-acre wildlife area, which provides one of the few public access points to the upper Verde and its floodplains, cliffs and adjacent uplands. Beneath cliffs that rise 100 to 300 feet above the river in some places, this lush riparian area is an important migration corridor for many bird species.

Wildlife to Watch

Resident species include golden and bald eagles, belted kingfisher and juniper titmouse. Migratory breeding birds include yellow-billed cuckoo, Cassin's kingbird and Bullock's oriole, while cooler months bring mountain and western bluebirds, sage thrasher and ferruginous hawk. Mammals include mule deer, javelina, beaver, coyote and river otter. This stretch of the Verde River is home to one of the most diverse assemblages of native fish in Arizona. Roundtail chub, Sonoran and desert suckers and longfin dace are the most common, but razorback sucker and spikedace may also be present. Lizards are highly visible during warmer months and eastern collared, greater earless, Clark's spiny and plateau lizards, and Gila spotted and desert grassland whiptails are commonly seen. Snakes of the area include the beautiful Sonoran mountain kingsnake, gopher snake, terrestrial gartersnake and Arizona black rattlesnake.

Audubon
IMPORTANT
BIRD AREAS

Trails

There are no official trails, but visitors may walk along three miles of the Verde River and one mile of Granite Creek, as well as along flood plain terraces and cliff faces adjacent to the river.

Site Notes Accessibility into the Verde River canyon is difficult due to steep and rocky terrain. High clearance vehicles are recommended.

Directions From State Hwy. 89 in Paulden, take Verde Ranch Road East (USFS 635) approximately 1 mile. Make a sharp right, cross the railroad tracks and make a sharp left. After crossing the railroad tracks, take the first dirt road to the right. Stay on this road for approximately 3 miles until you reach the Verde River canyon.

Contact Arizona Game and Fish Department; 928-692-7700 www.azgfd.gov/outdoor_recreation/wildlife_area_upper.shtml

Features restrooms, trash cans, overlooks, picnic tables, parking

Watson Lake Park 43

Description

This beautiful, deep-blue lake is surrounded by rocky formations known as the Granite Dells and a large cottonwood gallery. Several high points make for easy long-distance viewing with binoculars or spotting scopes. The 303-acre site is easily accessible by paved road.

Wildlife to Watch

A variety of birds, especially migratory and wintering waterfowl, can be seen along the lake and in the cottonwood gallery forest, home to an active great blue heron rookery and many pairs of attractive wood ducks. Bald eagle and osprey also occasionally stop by. Look beyond the lake and you may find mule deer, javelina and pronghorn. A variety of reptiles and amphibians inhabit the lake and its shores, including Clark's spiny lizard, plateau lizard, eastern collared lizard, terrestrial gartersnake, Woodhouse's toad and red-spotted toad.

Audubon
IMPORTANT
BIRD AREAS

Trails

The Discovery Trail is about one mile in length, connecting the park with the Peavine Trail through Watson Woods. Other trails lead throughout the park and into the Granite Dells.

Directions Located four miles north of Prescott on Hwy. 89.

Contact city of Prescott; 928-777-1564
www.cityofprescott.net/services/parks/parks.php

Features restrooms, trash cans, trails, bus/motorhome access, boat ramps, parking

Premier Sites

Great Sites

Other Sites

51

93

Bullhead City

49

Kingman

40

95

Lake Havasu City

45

89

Colorado River

Parker

53 54

Wickenburg

60

48

60

Wenden

47

Quartzsite

10

Buckeye

55 56

59

50

85

95

River & Desert

52 57

8

Gila Bend

44

58

Yuma

85

Ajo 46

River & Desert

The mighty Colorado River travels through seven states before entering Mexico. In the River and Desert region along the Arizona-California border, the river hosts a series of wildlife refuges. Here, the lower Colorado River brings water to the Mojave Desert, creating marshy oases for birds and animals. Other rivers in this region, including the Salt, Gila and Bill Williams Rivers, also provide welcome respite from harsh desert landscape.

Because of sparse vegetation, the geology is easily seen. In the mountains, look for a discrete break between the bedrock of the range and eroded sands and gravels at their bases. These "alluvial fans" form slowly, as rain washes weathered rock from the mountain slopes into the valleys.

PHOTO BY GARY R. HOVATTER

Clark's Grebe

PHOTO BY BRIAN E. SMALL

Description

Established in 1941, this wildlife refuge provides habitat for migratory birds and other wildlife along 30 miles of the lower Colorado River, including the last unchannelized section before the river enters Mexico. The lower Colorado River and associated marshlands here contrast sharply with the surrounding Sonoran Desert, which receives only 3½ inches of rain annually and is subject to extremely high summer temperatures.

Paloverde, Mesquite, Ironwood and Smoke Tree Observation Points offer beautiful views of the Colorado River valley. Follow the scenic Red Cloud Mine Road through the Sonoran Desert landscape to reach the observation points and the Painted Desert Trail. All of the observation points can be reached by vehicle, but if you intend to drive farther than the Painted Desert Trailhead, a 4-wheel drive vehicle is recommended. Check with the visitor center for road conditions.

Mining history and artifacts are scattered around the refuge in the mountainous areas, and petroglyphs can be found along the Colorado River.

Meers Point offers a quiet place to canoe and fish with shaded tables, toilets and a boat launch. Here, the refuge surrounds one of the few remaining "wild" places on the Colorado River, highly valued by boaters for its remote scenery.

Wildlife to Watch

Waterfowl are most abundant during winter, when large numbers of cinnamon and green-winged teals, gadwall, mallard and northern pintail use the refuge; other winter species include Canada goose, snow goose, sandhill crane and a

Premier
★ SITE ★

variety of herons, egrets and other waterbirds. White-faced ibis are almost always present. Migratory shorebirds such as Wilson's snipe, willet, sandpiper, yellowleg, black-necked stilt and others are common on mudflats following water fluctuations. During the summer months, look for resident species such as Gambel's quail, Clark's grebe, great blue heron, sora, mourning dove, cactus wren and muskrat. Osprey and other birds of prey can be found year-round. Burrowing owls are very common here; look for their burrows along the irrigation ditches that feed the wetlands within the refuge. In the upland areas, wildlife such as black-tailed jackrabbit, bighorn sheep, mule deer, coyote, tiger whiptail, desert spiny lizard, western diamond-backed rattlesnake and a variety of other reptiles can be viewed. Watch at dawn and dusk for bighorn sheep and mule deer heading to the river for a drink. Feral burros are also common to the site.

Trails

The self-guided Painted Desert Trail, a 1⅓-mile moderately strenuous loop, has outstanding views of the Sonoran Desert, ancient volcanic activity and the Colorado River. This scenic trail leads through a rainbow of colors left by 20–30 million year-old volcanic activity and features a panoramic view of the Colorado River valley.

Site Notes	Observation points are accessible by car; the observation tower near the visitor center provides universal accessibility. Kiosks provide interpretive information about the refuge. Guided hikes are offered during the winter.
Size	25,768 acres
Directions	From Yuma, take State Hwy. 95 north to Martinez Lake Road. Turn left (west) and travel 10 miles to Red Cloud Mine Road. Turn right (north) and follow the brown refuge signs approximately 3½ miles to the visitor center.
Nearest Town	Yuma (40 miles), Martinez Lake (3 miles)
Ownership	U.S. Fish and Wildlife Service
Contact	928-783-3371 www.fws.gov/southwest/refuges/arizona/imperial.html
Features	restrooms, trash cans/recycling, trails, observation points, interpretive signs, brochure/bird species lists, visitor center, drinking water, bus/motorhome access, boat ramps, parking, observation tower

RIVER & DESERT ■ Imperial National Wildlife Refuge

Premier ★ SITE ★

Cactus Wren

PHOTO BY BRUCE D. TAUBERT

Sora

PHOTO BY BRUCE D. TAUBERT

Premier
★ SITE ★

Bill Williams RIver National Wildlife Refuge

PHOTO BY WILLIAM RADKE

Description

With its majestic rock cliffs, its ribbon of cool water running through classic Sonoran Desert, and its cattail-filled marsh harboring rails and waterfowl, Bill Williams River National Wildlife Refuge offers a little bit of everything for both wildlife and people. The refuge holds one of the last stands of natural cottonwood-willow forest along the lower Colorado River. Dramatic vistas include volcanic cliffs, Lake Havasu and the Bill Williams Delta Marsh. The river is named for a mountain man who traveled through much of Arizona in the early 1800s.

Wildlife to Watch

The rare riparian habitat draws a variety of migratory birds to nest among the lush vegetation such as Lucy's and yellow warblers, yellow-breasted chat, Bell's vireo, vermilion and brown-crested flycatchers, hooded and Bullock's orioles, blue grosbeak and summer tanager. About a dozen Yuma clapper rails spend the summer months in the cattails of the marsh, although they are more likely heard than seen. Willow flycatcher and yellow-billed cuckoo nest on the refuge in the willow and tamarisk trees lining the river. Crisscrossing tracks in the sand chronicle the nighttime excursions of desert cottontail, javelina and mule deer, as well as predatory coyote and bobcat. Reptiles and amphibians also inhabit the refuge and may be seen throughout the warmer months. Species to watch for include common kingsnake, long-nosed snake, Sonoran mud turtle, desert spiny and ornate tree lizards, and red-spotted and Great Plains toads.

Great
▲ SITE ▲

Trails

The ¼-mile interpretive trail is universally accessible with fishing access; additional ¼-mile hiking trail. Brochures for self-guided auto tour and canoe route are available at office.

Site Notes	Check at office for conditions of refuge road as flooding is a concern.
Size	6,105 acres
Directions	From Parker, go 18 miles north on Hwy. 95. From Lake Havasu City, go 15 miles south on Hwy. 95. Refuge office is between mile markers 160 and 161 on lake side of highway.
Nearest Town	Parker/Lake Havasu City
Ownership	U.S. Fish and Wildlife Service
Contact	928-667-4144 www.fws.gov/southwest/refuges/arizona/billwill.html
Features	restrooms, trash cans, trails, overlooks, interpretive signs, brochure/species list, visitor center, drinking water, bus/motorhome access, canoe/kayak launch facility, parking, fishing docks

Yellow-breasted Chat

PHOTO BY TOM VEZO

RIVER & DESERT ■ *Bill Williams River National Wildlife Refuge*

Great
▲ SITE ▲

A protected home for North America's rarest large land mammal

Cabeza Prieta National Wildlife Refuge

PHOTO BY JIM HEDRICK

Description

A remote, dry section of the Sonoran Desert on the border between the United States and Mexico, this refuge is home to the Sonoran pronghorn and other desert-dwelling wildlife. Originally established in 1939 to protect a dwindling population of bighorn sheep, the refuge has since expanded its mission to include protection of an entire desert ecosystem, including excellent examples of Sonoran Desert plants and animals.

The Child's Mountain Watchable Wildlife Area near the refuge headquarters offers visitors an excellent overview of the refuge and is accessible to visitors with 2-wheel drive vehicles, but a locked gate limits access to refuge-sponsored activities. More than 90% of the refuge was designated as wilderness in 1990, so vehicle access through the area is limited to three unimproved roads that require high-clearance, 4-wheel drive vehicles. This is one of the driest parts of the state; the refuge experiences summer temperatures that can easily exceed 115°.

Wildlife to Watch

This refuge offers good opportunities for viewing a variety of Sonoran Desert plants and animals. Spring offers the best time to see migrating birds and wildflower blooms, which can be spectacular following adequate winter rains. The taller trees and denser vegetation found along dry washes often attract an amazing variety of desert migrating songbirds from March through early May. Common wildlife includes the Gila woodpecker, curve-billed thrasher, cactus wren, white-winged dove, verdin and an occasional Harris's hawk. A variety of migrating birds of prey can be abundant, especially during autumn. Commonly seen reptiles include the zebra-tailed lizard, desert iguana, tiger whiptail, western patch-nosed snake, coachwhip and sidewinder. Bighorn sheep and the rare Sonoran pronghorn are present on the refuge but are difficult to find and observe. Most of the refuge is closed from March 15–July 15 to protect the fawning pronghorn. A small pond at refuge headquarters provides an opportunity to view the unique Quitobaquito pupfish, a fish having remarkable abilities to survive hot water temperatures and high mineral concentrations.

Trails

Short, gravel-surfaced trails are located at refuge headquarters and on Child's Mountain Watchable Wildlife Area. Camping and backcountry hiking are permitted on the refuge, but no improved trails exist through this wilderness. This is rugged country requiring backpackers to be exceptionally physically fit, knowledgeable about desert travel, and able to carry ample water. Potable water is unavailable on the refuge.

Site Notes Permit required. Limited public access—check access prior to visit. All visitors must obtain a free permit to enter the refuge because of the adjoining Barry M. Goldwater Air Force Range; military aircraft train adjacent to and in the airspace over the refuge. Visitors should contact the refuge headquarters in Ajo for area information, current conditions, visitor permits and information concerning staff and docent-led trips on the refuge in the winter. Office hours are 7:30 a.m. to 12 p.m. and 1 p.m. to 4:30 p.m. Monday through Friday, closed weekends and holidays.

Border Notes The refuge borders Mexico for 65 miles of remote, wild lands. Over the last several years the refuge has experienced a large upsurge in illegal activity, including drug smuggling and illegal immigrant crossings. Border Patrol and other agency law enforcement officers patrol the refuge and engage in interdiction operations. Refuge visitors are advised to use caution and common sense when camping, encountering unknown individuals, or leaving a vehicle for extended periods.

Size 860,010 acres

Directions From Tucson take Exit 99 on I-19 and drive 115 miles west on State Route 86 to Why and then 10 miles northwest on State Route 85 to Ajo. From Gila Bend take Exit 115 on I-8 and drive 42 miles south on state route 85 to Ajo. Refuge headquarters is located in Ajo at 1611 North Second Street.

Nearest Town Ajo

Ownership U.S. Fish and Wildlife Service

Contact 520-387-6483; www.fws.gov/southwest/refuges/Arizona/cabeza.html

Features visitor center, brochure/species list, drinking water, restrooms, shade ramada, parking, overlook, interpretive signs

Great
▲ SITE ▲

Cibola National Wildlife Refuge

PHOTO BY BILL SEESE/USFWS

Description

In the floodplain of the lower Colorado River and surrounded by a fringe of desert ridges and washes, this refuge encompasses both the historic Colorado River channel as well as a channelized portion constructed in the late 1960s. Several backwaters are home to many wildlife species that reside in this portion of the Sonoran Desert. Because of the river's life-sustaining water, wildlife here survives in an environment that reaches 120° in the summer and receives an average of only two inches of rain per year. The river corridor is framed by outstanding desert views with rugged mountain backdrops.

Wildlife to Watch

Over 288 species of birds have been found at Cibola. Gambel's quail, greater roadrunner, mourning and white-winged doves, phainopepla, sandhill crane, American white pelican, osprey, vermilion flycatcher, blue grosbeak, bald eagle, willow flycatcher and Yuma clapper rail are among the birds that use the refuge. Thousands of Canada geese migrate to Cibola in the winter; about 85% of Arizona's wintering goose population resides here. These are often joined by smaller numbers of snow, Ross's and greater white-fronted geese, as well as occasional tundra swan.

It is not uncommon to see burrowing owl, mule deer, bobcat and coyote, particularly while driving the auto tour loop in the early morning or evening. Many waterbirds nest in the backwaters of the river; it is common to see western and Clark's grebe young riding on their parents' backs in Cibola Lake

RIVER & DESERT ■ *Cibola National Wildlife Refuge*

Great
▲ SITE ▲

during the spring, a great blue heron and egret rookery, or nesting mourning and white-winged doves, barn owl, burrowing owl and American kestrel. White-faced ibis have also nested here on occasion.

Trails

The 3-mile auto tour loop (also known as Canada Goose Drive) allows access through the refuge. Along this drive is the Nature Trail, a 1-mile loop through three different habitats; cottonwood, mesquite and willow. Halfway around the trail, winter visitors may view thousands of Canada geese, snow geese, various duck species and sandhill cranes in a 20-acre pond from an elevated observation deck. The Nature Trail is dirt and gravel and can be accessed with some difficulty.

Size	18,000 acres
Directions	From Blythe, CA, go approximately 5 miles west on I-10 to Neighbours Boulevard/Hwy. 78 exit. Go south on Neighbours for 17 miles to the Cibola Bridge. After crossing the bridge, continue south for 3½ miles to headquarters.
Nearest Town	Blythe, California
Ownership	U.S. Fish and Wildlife Service
Contact	928-857-3253 www.fws.gov/southwest/refuges/CibolaNWR/index.html
Features	restrooms, trails, overlooks, interpretive signs, brochure/bird species list, visitor center, drinking water, bus/motorhome access, boat ramps, photo blinds, observation deck

Canada Geese

PHOTO BY BRUCE D. TAUBERT

Hassayampa River Preserve
On Arizona's state register of historic places

Hassayampa River Preserve

PHOTO BY GEORGE ANDREJKO

Description

The Hassayampa River Preserve has been a nature lover's and birder's paradise since it was purchased by The Nature Conservancy in 1986. Once part of the Frederick Brill Ranch, the preserve is now listed on Arizona's State Register of Historic Places.

The preserve features desert cottonwood/willow riparian forest, desert fan palms, plus Sonoran Desert species such as saguaro, barrel and cholla cactus, mesquite, paloverde and spring wildflowers. The preserve provides habitat for more than 280 resident and migratory bird species.

Wildlife to Watch

The marshy pond habitat attracts an impressive array of water birds such as great blue and green herons, and pied-billed grebe. Some of Arizona's rarest raptors perch atop the massive trees and dead snags along the river, such as the zone-tailed hawk, common black-hawk and the more common Harris's and Cooper's hawks. Lucky birders may sight a red-shouldered hawk or the elusive yellow-billed cuckoo. The large willows and cottonwoods around the pond provide important nesting habitat for the willow flycatcher and brief stop-over habitat for migrating warblers, vireos, tanagers, grosbeaks and orioles. Several bird species that are characteristic of southeastern Arizona have recently expanded their summer range northward to include the preserve, including gray hawk, tropical and thick-billed kingbirds and northern beardless-tyrannulet.

Great
▲ SITE ▲

Other birds include Gambel's quail, red-tailed hawk, Gila and ladder-backed woodpeckers, black phoebe, verdin, cactus wren, curve-billed thrasher, phainopepla, Abert's towhee, brown-crested flycatcher, Lucy's and yellow warblers and yellow-breasted chat. During the spring and summer, bird feeders and flowering plants in front of the visitor center regularly attract Anna's, black-chinned and Costa's hummingbirds. You may also see mule deer, javelina, Clark's spiny lizard, ornate tree lizard, Gilbert's skink and ring-necked snake.

Trails

Five mostly level trails, each approximately ½ mile long.

Site Notes	Fee site. The preserve occasionally closes during the summer months due to fire danger. The Visitors Center provides maps, trail guides and loaner binoculars, as well as a student guide for children.
Size	600 acres
Directions	Hassayampa River Preserve is located on Hwy. 60, 3 miles southeast of Wickenburg. Entrance is on the west side of the highway near mile marker 114.
Nearest Town	Wickenburg
Ownership	The Nature Conservancy
Contact	928-684-2772 www.nature.org/wherewework/northamerica/states/arizona/preserves/art1970.html
Features	restrooms, trash cans, trails, overlooks, interpretive signs, brochure/species list, visitor center, drinking water, bus/motorhome access, picnic area, parking, photo blinds, bird feeding stations

Vermilion Flycatcher   *PHOTO BY BRUCE D. TAUBERT*

RIVER & DESERT ■ *Hassayampa River Preserve*

Great
▲ SITE ▲

Backwaters of the lower Colorado River

Havasu National WIldlife Refuge

PHOTO BY MATT SHERRELL/USFWS

Description

The waters of the lower Colorado River flow through Topock Gorge and Topock Marsh in this wildlife refuge near the Arizona-California border. Topock Gorge is one of the most scenic portions of the Colorado River south of the Grand Canyon. Rugged desert mountains and colorful rocky cliffs give visitors a beautiful backdrop for wildlife viewing.

President Franklin D. Roosevelt created this refuge in 1941 to provide habitat for migratory waterfowl. The marsh and gorge represent over 40% of the remaining backwaters of the lower Colorado River. The refuge protects 300 miles of shoreline from Needles, California to Lake Havasu City, Arizona.

Indian petroglyphs in Topock Gorge trace the stories of early peoples who lived along the river. A few old mines tell a more recent tale of nineteenth-century gold prospectors hoping to strike it rich.

Wildlife to Watch

From bighorn sheep to the willow flycatcher, wildlife at the refuge rely on the life-giving waters of the lower Colorado River. Birders come to the refuge for some of the best birding on the lower Colorado.

Popular birding locations on the refuge are Pintail Slough, Fivemile Landing and Catfish Paradise, which can be accessed from County Route 1. Each of these sites has parking and can easily be toured on foot. A viewing tower overlooking the Bermuda Pasture can be accessed by Levee Road.

Along with many species of ducks and geese, you may also see Clark's and western grebes, Anna's hummingbird and Abert's towhee. The refuge shelters Canada and snow geese and ducks each winter, along with white-faced ibis and American white pelicans. Nesting Yuma clapper and Virginia rails, common moorhen, least bittern and marsh wren use dense cattail habitat. Isolated stands of willow, cottonwood and taller tamarisk attract migrating flycatchers, warblers, vireos, tanagers, grosbeaks and orioles.

Common to the refuge are bighorn sheep, black-tailed jackrabbit and various species of mice and wood (pack) rats. Along the river, songbirds use the shelter of Fremont cottonwoods, Goodding's willow, and honey and screwbean mesquite.

The canyon walls also provide habitat for a variety of reptile and amphibian species, including Great Basin collared lizard, common chuckwalla, rosy boa, gopher snake, speckled rattlesnake and red-spotted toad.

Trails

Visitors are welcome to walk on over five miles of service roads, including South Dike, New South Dike and in Pintail Slough.

Size	37,515 acres
Directions	Topock Marsh: From Bullhead City, take Hwy. 95 approximately 15 miles south, turn east on Courtwright Rd and drive approximately 3 miles. Topock Marsh will be on your right for the next 10 miles.
	The Topock Gorge Unit lies on the Colorado River beginning at the I-40 Bridge and stretching 18 miles south to the north end of Lake Havasu
Nearest Town	Golden Shores
Ownership	U.S. Fish and Wildlife Service
Contact	760-326-3853 www.fws.gov/soutwest/refuges/ arizona/havasu/
Features	restrooms, trash cans, lookouts, interpretive signs, brochure/bird species list, bus/motorhome access, boat ramps, parking

Least Bittern   PHOTO BY E. J. PEIKER

Great
▲ SITE ▲

Kofa National Wildlife Refuge

PHOTO BY SUSANNA HENRY/USFWS

Description

The pristine beauty of the rugged Sonoran Desert is showcased at the Kofa National Wildlife Refuge, where broad, gently sloping foothills nestle beneath sharp, needlepoint peaks. The rugged and scenic Kofa and Castle Dome mountains, along with portions of the Tank, New Water and Little Horn mountains, dominate the landscape.

Landforms reflect outstanding examples of geologic uplift and a variety of different rock types. Native plant species include a few relict stands of California fan palms, Kofa Mountain barberry and scrub oak. Visitors who venture higher into the Kofa Mountains see desert plants that have adapted to the rise in elevation, including bear grass and desert agave. If winter rains allow, tremendous wildflower displays can burst forth in spring.

The stone and mortar Kofa Cabin, built by the Arizona Conservation Corps in the 1930s, is a popular destination for visitors, who may also see evidence of past mining for gold, silver, manganese and lead as they explore the refuge. The refuge's name, Kofa, is a contraction of the famous "King of Arizona" mine's name.

Wildlife to Watch

This refuge protects 600 to 800 bighorn sheep that live in the rugged Kofa and Castle Dome Mountains. You may also see mule deer in the refuge.

Great
▲ SITE ▲

Look for wildlife burrows while driving the refuge roads; these are home to ground squirrel, pocket mice, woodrat and kangaroo rat.

The desert tortoise is one of the longest living creatures in the United States. Other interesting species include the rosy boa, western shovel-nosed snake, five species of rattlesnakes, desert iguana, Sonoran Desert toad and the red-spotted toad. Birds include red-tailed hawk, golden eagle, ash-throated flycatcher, loggerhead shrike, cactus and canyon wrens, phainopepla, Scott's oriole and curve-billed thrasher. Among the low oaks and dense desert scrub at higher elevations, hikers will find isolated nesting populations of blue-gray gnatcatcher, canyon towhee, and black-chinned and rufous-crowned sparrows.

Trails

There is a 1-mile trail at Palm Canyon. Strong hikers may continue on from the palm viewing area into the upper reaches of Palm Canyon for an up-close look at these unique plants.

Site Notes	Kofa was included in desert military training exercises during World War II. Unexploded ordinance may be encountered during cross-country hiking. Picking up items that appear to be military hardware could be hazardous to your health. Avoid old mine shafts that may be unstable and hazardous to visitors.
Size	664,327 acres, of which 547,719 acres (82%) is wilderness
Directions	There are 4 marked entrances to the refuge off U.S. Hwy. 95 between Yuma and Quartzsite and another at Exit 45 on I-10 (Vicksburg Road). Travel south on the Vicksburg Road to reach the refuge.
Nearest Town	Yuma and Quartzsite
Ownership	U.S. Fish and Wildlife Service
Contact	928-783-7861 www.fws.gov/southwest/ refuges/arizona/kofa.html
Features	trails, interpretive signs, brochure/species list, visitor center, parking, bus/motorhome access, photo blinds

Desert Tortoise   PHOTO BY GEORGE ANDREJKO

Great
▲ SITE ▲

RIVER & DESERT ■ *Lake Mead National Recreation Area*

Lake Mead National Recreation Area

PHOTO BY GEORGE ANDREJKO

Description

Lake Mead National Recreation Area is a startling contrast of desert and water, mountains and canyons, primitive backcountry and busy marinas. Lake Mead and Lake Mohave were created by dams on the Colorado River as it flows through one of the hottest, driest regions on earth. The quiet, stark beauty of the Mojave Desert with its dramatic exposed geology and the surprising abundance of specially adapted plants and animals offers a variety of experiences for everyone.

Here, three of America's four desert ecosystems—the Mojave, Great Basin and Sonoran Deserts—meet. Striking and dramatic physical features include deep canyons, dry washes, sheer cliffs, distant mountain ranges, lakes, colorful soils and rock formations, and mosaics of different vegetation.

Wildlife to Watch

Small herds of bighorn sheep can be seen along the ridges and canyons. Other mammals that may be observed include various species of rodents and bats, including Arizona, brush and pocket mouse.

More than 240 different kinds of birds have been recorded. Due to the great summer heat, most birds in the region are visitors, coming during the fall, winter and spring months. Gambel's quail, rock wren, verdin and black-tailed gnatcatcher are here year round however, as are a wide range of birds of prey, such as great horned owl, red-tailed hawk, golden eagle, American kestrel and

Great
▲ SITE ▲

peregrine falcon. These large bodies of open water attract several species of loons, grebes, mergansers and other diving ducks during the winter months, although western grebe are often observed throughout the year. Visitors may encounter a variety of reptiles and amphibians, including long-nosed leopard lizard, Great Basin collared lizard, desert iguana, common chuckwalla, the small and secretive desert night lizard, gopher snake, long-nosed snake, Mohave rattlesnake, red-spotted toad, Great Plains toad and Woodhouse's toad.

Trails

Main hiking areas are: Arizona Hot Springs (6-mile trail); Railroad Hiking Trail (2⅗ miles with tunnels); River Mountain Loop Trail (10 miles); Northshore Hikes (five hikes from ½ to 1¼ miles); Katherine Hikes (three short hikes); and Grapevine Canyon (¼-mile hike to petroglyphs, further into canyon for rock dwellings).

Site Notes	Summer temperatures reach 120° in the shade.
Size	1,495,664 acres
Directions	From Boulder City, Nevada, take U.S. Hwy. 93 to Willow Beach Road and Willow Beach Road west toward Willow Beach.
Nearest Town	Boulder City, NV
Ownership	National Park Service
Contact	702-293-8907 www.nps.gov/lame/
Features	restrooms, trash cans, trails, lookouts, interpretive signs, brochure/species list, visitor center, drinking water, bus/motorhome access, boat ramps, parking

Gambel's Quail   PHOTO BY PAUL BERQUIST

Great
▲ SITE ▲

Mittry Lake Wildlife Area

PHOTO BY GEORGE ANDREJKO

Description

Mittry Lake is a 400-acre oxbow of the lower Colorado River, with a well-developed wetland and marsh habitat. Wonderful views of three surrounding mountain ranges combine with excellent waterfowl and wildlife viewing. In winter, up to 10,000 waterfowl may be present. This is one of the most accessible settings for wildlife viewing in the Colorado River floodplain.

Wildlife to Watch

A variety of birds such as the yellow-billed cuckoo, summer tanager and willow flycatcher use the area. Yuma clapper rail nest on site. Surveys have revealed California black rail and Virginia rail nesting along the shore. The marsh also supports nesting populations of marsh wren, American coot, common moorhen, least bittern and pied-billed grebe.

Winter users include many duck species, sora, American white pelican, double-crested cormorant and northern harrier. During migration, thousands of swallows are sometimes observed coming to roost for the night in the marsh vegetation. Resident bird species include black-crowned night-heron, great blue heron, snowy egret, osprey and many others. Mammals include mule deer, javelina and bobcat. Tiger whiptail, ornate tree lizard, common kingsnake, western diamond-backed rattlesnake and a variety of other reptiles can be viewed.

Audubon
IMPORTANT
BIRD AREAS

RIVER & DESERT ■ *Mittry Lake Wildlife Area*

Great
▲ SITE ▲

Trails

No formal trails.

Site Notes Watch for wild burros along the paved roads. Designated seasonal closure areas provide sanctuary for migrating waterfowl.

Size 3,575 acres

Directions From Yuma, take State Hwy. 95 north. Turn north onto Avenue 7E and travel approximately 9 miles to the lake. You will pass Laguna Dam to get to the lake. Or, take Hwy. 95 north to the Imperial Dam Road; turn left (west) on Imperial Dam Road. Pass the Yuma Proving Grounds Headquarters, cross the Gila Gravity Main Canal, and turn left onto the canal road. Follow the wildlife area signs.

Nearest Town Yuma

Ownership Bureau of Land Management; cooperatively managed by Arizona Game and Fish Department, Bureau of Land Management and Bureau of Reclamation

Contact 928-342-0091; 928-317-3200
www.azgfd.gov/outdoor_recreation/wildlife_area_mittry_lake.shtml

Features restrooms, trash cans, trails, brochure/bird species list, bus/motorhome access, boat ramps, parking, boat dock, ramada w/picnic tables, campgrounds, fishing jetties

Marsh Wren PHOTO BY BRIAN E. SMALL

Great
▲ SITE ▲

Alamo Lake State Park 53

Description

Stark desert beauty reflects in the waters of Alamo Lake, located on the Bill Williams River where the Big Sandy and Santa Maria Rivers join. Surrounded by cactus-dotted mountains, this remote but well-visited park of 2,858 acres lies at 1,300 feet elevation. If winter rains are adequate, there is potential for tremendous displays of wildflowers in early spring, and the lake attracts a variety of wildlife year-round.

Wildlife to Watch

In the winter, the lake has high populations of grebes and waterfowl, including several species of teal, mallard, ruddy duck, bufflehead, common goldeneye and eared grebe. Year round, see waterbirds such as American coot, western and Clark's grebes, great egret, black-crowned night-heron, great blue heron, double-crested cormorant, American white pelican and an occasional brown pelican. During migration, gulls, terns and shorebirds can also be observed. Bald eagle have nested at the upper end of the lake and below the dam. You may also see gray fox, coyote, mule deer, javelina, bighorn sheep and feral burros.

Site Notes Fee site. Use caution if venturing off the main roads; dirt roads can quickly turn into rugged jeep trails.

Directions Go 38 miles north of Wenden on Alamo Road (off Hwy. 60).

Contact Arizona State Parks; 928-669-2088
www.azstateparks.com/Parks/parkhtml/alamo.html

Features restrooms, trash cans, overlooks, visitor center, drinking water, bus/motorhome access, boat ramps, parking, picnic areas, campground

Alamo Lake Wildlife Area 54

Description

Magnificent scenic views of the surrounding mountains and Sonoran Desert uplands are available from almost every part of the 20,000-acre wildlife area. The wildlife area is one of The Nature Conservancy's Sustainable Rivers Project sites.

Wildlife to Watch

The area's lush wetland and streamside vegetation attracts a wide range of wildlife species. Wildlife may be viewed from vehicles on designated roads and trails, by foot on trails and by boat on Alamo Lake.

Waterfowl and shorebirds frequent the area; western grebe reproduce on Alamo Lake. Bald eagle nest here, as do willow flycatcher, yellow-billed cuckoo, black-chinned hummingbird, Bell's vireo, crissal thrasher, phainopepla, Bullock's oriole and lesser goldfinch. Mule deer, javelina, bobcat, coyote and desert cottontail are common. Common reptiles and amphibians include common kingsnake, long-nosed snake, Sonoran mud turtle, desert spiny and ornate tree lizards, and red-spotted and Great Plains toads. Look for feral burros, especially in summer when they come to the water.

Audubon
IMPORTANT
BIRD AREAS

Directions Take Alamo Dam Road north from Wenden about 35 miles or Alamo Road west from U.S. Route 93 near Congress.

Contact Arizona Game and Fish Department; 928-342-0091; www.azgfd.gov/outdoor_recreation/wildlife_area_alamo_lake.shtml

Features trails, brochure/species list, boat ramps, campgrounds

Arlington Wildlife Area   55

Description

The 1,000-acre Arlington Wildlife Area is made up of open ponds, approximately four miles of river channel along the west bank of the Gila River, marshlands and stands of high quality willow riparian habitat. Three ponds offer different types of aquatic and marshland habitats. The pond areas offer excellent viewing of marshland wildlife during fall and spring.

Wildlife to Watch

The open water ponds can attract numerous waterfowl, herons, egrets and shorebirds during migration and winter. Yuma clapper rail, common moorhen, pied-billed grebe, least bittern, common yellowthroat, Abert's towhee, song sparrow, and yellow-headed and red-winged blackbirds nest in the wetland habitat along with mourning and white-winged doves, Gambel's quail, verdin and black-tailed gnatcatcher in the nearby trees and shrubs. Bobcats are surprisingly common along this section of the Gila River, and mule deer, javelina, coyote and raccoon are also seen with regularity. The area provides habitat for numerous amphibians and reptiles that may be seen during warmer months.

Audubon
IMPORTANT
BIRD AREAS

Directions Exit I-10 at exit 112 (near Buckeye) and go south on SR 85 about 5 miles. Exit State Hwy. 85 to west onto Old US 80 and follow about 15 miles to Arlington School Road. Turn right (south) and go to end of pavement at Desert Rose Lane. Follow the farm field road ½ mile further south along the same alignment as Arlington School Road to the wildlife area entrance.

Contact Arizona Game and Fish Department; 480-981-9400 www.azgfd.gov/outdoor_recreation/wildlife_area_arlington.shtml

Features parking

RIVER & DESERT ■ Other Sites

Other sites

Description

Offering outstanding views over the Gila River valley from Monument Hill, this wildlife area received its name because of its proximity to the spot where the township and range coordinate system for mapping Arizona is centered. Visitors to this 200-acre area enjoy its riparian and marshland habitats, a welcome natural break in an increasingly urban landscape.

Wildlife to Watch

Visitors can see herons, egrets, osprey, double-crested cormorant and other fish-eating birds. Also relatively easy to view are numerous birds of prey, as well as black vulture, white-winged and mourning doves, Gambel's quail, American coot, common moorhen, Abert's towhee and occasionally American white pelican. Huge nesting colonies of cliff swallows can be found under the bridge during the spring and summer. During the winter, large numbers of warblers in the area include the less common black-throated gray warbler, Townsend's warbler, or even rarer species. Mammals include beaver, bobcat, javelina and desert kangaroo rat. Numerous reptiles and amphibians include tiger whiptail, common side-blotched lizard, common kingsnake, checkered gartersnake, Couch's spadefoot and Great Plains toad.

Audubon
IMPORTANT
BIRD AREAS

Directions From Avondale, go south on Avondale Boulevard to bridge over Gila River. Parking available at NE corner of bridge and at first entrance to Phoenix International Raceway grounds.

Contact Arizona Game and Fish Department; 480-981-9400
www.azgfd.gov/outdoor_recreation/wildlife_area_base.shtml

Features parking, overlooks

Betty's Kitchen National Recreation Trail   57

Description

The Betty's Kitchen National Recreation Trail winds through dense riparian vegetation past a fishing pier and over a rugged metal bridge. The 10-acre site is next to historic Laguna Dam, the first dam built on the Colorado River.

Wildlife to Watch

Waterfowl visit during the winter and migratory birds visit during spring, fall and early winter. The best seasons to visit are between March and May, and from late August through October when impressive numbers of migratory species such as flycatchers, warblers, vireos, tanagers, buntings, grosbeaks and sparrows can be found. Other wildlife includes desert cottontail, rock squirrel, desert spiny lizard, ornate tree lizard, tiger whiptail, common kingsnake and western diamond-backed rattlesnake.

Other sites

Trails

A ½-mile interpretive loop trail provides universal accessibility.

Directions From Yuma, go 7 miles east on U.S. Hwy. 95 to Avenue 7E (Laguna Dam Road). Turn north and follow this road for 9 miles past Laguna Dam. Turn left and follow the signs.

Contact Bureau of Land Management; 928-317-3200
www.blm.gov/az/trails/bettykitchtrail.htm

Features restrooms, trash cans, trails, overlooks, interpretive signs, bus/motorhome access, parking

Quigley Wildlife Area   58

Description

The Quigley Wildlife Area encompasses a remnant slough of the Gila River in the middle of the Sonoran Desert, one of the driest areas in North America. The 612-acre wildlife area provides magnificent views across the floodplain to the Castle Dome and Paloma mountain ranges.

Wildlife to Watch

Several rarely seen birds including the Yuma clapper, least bittern and marsh wren nest here, although they are more often heard than seen. Concentrations of wintering waterfowl and shorebirds can be seen, along with significant numbers of migratory song birds. Look for mourning and white-winged doves, lesser nighthawk, black phoebe, Gambel's quail, greater roadrunner, snow goose, Abert's towhee and osprey. Sandhill crane are sometimes observed during fall and early winter.

Audubon
IMPORTANT
BIRD AREAS

Directions From Yuma, take I-8 east towards Phoenix. Exit at Avenue 40E or Tacna (exit 42), turn north and cross the railroad tracks. Go north for 1⅓ miles then west onto a dirt road for ½ mile to the mesa on the southernmost boundary overlooking the ponds.

Contact Arizona Game and Fish Department; 928-342-0091
www.azgfd.gov/outdoor_recreation/wildlife_area_quigley.shtml

Features trails, viewing platform, parking

Robbins Butte Wildlife Area   59

Description

Standing atop Robbins Butte, one can see the Gila River corridor winding through the desert below. The Gila's diverse habitats draw large populations of resident and migratory wildlife to this area.

Ruins and petroglyphs document the importance of this area to human habitation and farming for the last 500 years. Today, the 3,000-acre Robbins Butte Wildlife Area is managed with modern fields growing crops for wildlife and a diverse mix of native habitats to encourage wildlife and wildlife-oriented recreation.

Wildlife to Watch

Mourning and white-winged doves, Gambel's quail, coyote, desert cottontail and black-tailed jackrabbit are abundant, along with javelina, mule deer and bobcat. Resident songbirds include black and Say's phoebes, ash-throated flycatcher, loggerhead shrike, phainopepla, verdin, crissal thrasher, Abert's towhee and black-throated sparrow. Bird diversity and abundance increase dramatically during the winter, with the local Gila River Christmas Bird Count regularly exceeding 140 species, with over 45,000 individuals often compiled. Birds of prey are also common during the fall and winter, particularly near agricultural fields. White-tailed kite are occasionally observed. Gila monster and a wide variety of reptiles are frequently encountered in season.

Audubon
IMPORTANT
BIRD AREAS

Site Notes Several species of rattlesnakes can be found in and around Robbins Butte Wildlife Area. Warm weather visitors should take appropriate precautions.

Directions Exit I-10 at exit 112 (near Buckeye) and go south on SR 85 for 6 miles. Exit State Hwy. 85 to west at milepost 147, the entrance to the wildlife area.

Contact Arizona Game and Fish Department; 480-981-9400 www.azgfd.gov/outdoor_recreation/wildlife_area_robbins.shtml

Features parking, primitive campgrounds

Arizona Quail

Arizona is blessed with a diversity of quail species due to the wide array of habitats and the many desert divisions and transition zones found within its borders. Four native and one introduced species occur in Arizona: California, Gambel's (at left), masked bobwhite, Montezuma (or Mearns') and scaled.

Gambel's quail are a symbol of the Sonoran Desert, but can be found in appropriate mixed shrub habitats within all the desert divisions of Arizona. This is a well known species to Arizona residents and visitors alike, easily recognized by its plumed topknot and familiar call. One of the most common birds in the Sonoran Desert, abundance and distribution of this species is directly affected by good "winter" (October through March) precipitation.

Arizona represents the westernmost natural range of scaled quail. Dark bordered feathers present a fish scale appearance on the breast of this bird, leading to its common name. Found in abundance only within Chihuahuan Desert grassland and associated upland habitats of southeastern Arizona, this species is often referred to as "cottontop" owing to its white-topped crest.

Few people are ever fortunate enough to observe Montezuma or Mearns' quail in the wild. Low observability is not due to small population size; rather to this species' habits, cryptic coloration and the habitat it prefers. Often called "fool's quail" by early explorers, they crouch when threatened and allow for a very close approach before flushing. Given the cryptic nature of this species, this strategy serves them well in avoiding potential predators. Montezuma quail are found primarily in southeastern Arizona "Sky Islands" in oak-grassland savannah habitats. A lucky observer may also encounter this bird in grassland-savannah habitats associated with the Mogollon Rim. Tall native bunchgrasses are a necessary component of Montezuma quail habitat.

Masked bobwhites, a subspecies of the Northern bobwhite, remain naturally in the wild only in northern Sonora, Mexico. However, masked bobwhites historically extended into the Altar Valley and possibly the Santa Cruz River Valley prior to the late 1800s–early 1900s. The U.S. Fish and Wildlife Service has been attempting to reestablish masked bobwhites on the Buenos Aires National Wildlife Refuge (located in the Altar Valley), with some limited success, primarily due to relocation of wild masked bobwhites from Mexico.

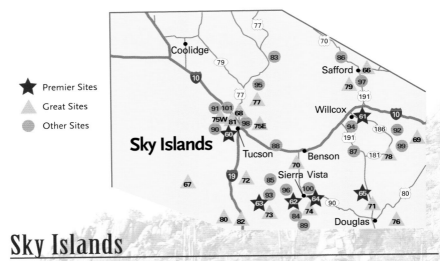

Sky Islands

Southern Arizona is characterized by "basin and range" topography, which forms as the Earth's surface is slowly pulled apart. In such areas, surface rocks break along faults. Some blocks of rock rise, while others drop, forming mountain ranges and intervening basins or valleys.

The Basin and Range geological province reaches its climax in the Sky Islands region, where mountains in excess of 6,000 feet elevation are common. The geology is quite complex, with various kinds of rock forming the different ranges. Like islands in an ocean of grassland and desert, the mountains offer shelter from summer's heat. Perennial streams water gentle forests of sycamore, cottonwood and other trees, creating a lush haven for wildlife.

PHOTO BY BRUCE D. TAUBERT

Costa's Hummingbird

PHOTO BY CHARLES W. MELTON

Description

Located in Tucson Mountain Park and adjacent to Saguaro National Monument in one of the most pristine and lush saguaro-paloverde forests of Arizona, the Arizona-Sonora Desert Museum offers spectacular wildlife viewing and mountain scenery. This world-renowned facility combines elements of a zoo, natural history museum and botanical garden. Its unique approach interprets the complete natural history of the Sonoran Desert region and its adjacent ecosystems. A broad range of interpretive activities is offered, including venomous reptile demonstrations, raptor free-flight demonstrations from October to April, bird walks, summertime butterfly walks and a variety of self-guided walks and activities. The museum also sponsors scientific research and conservation. This is a perfect place for photographers to capture photos of a wide variety of captive Southwest species in natural-looking settings. Due to the lush environment created at the museum, photographers can also expect to obtain photos of wild animals in their native habitat.

Wildlife to Watch

The museum displays over 300 species of animals and more than 200 species of plants native to the Sonoran Desert in naturalistic habitat settings. Among the highlights are two aviaries, the Desert Loop Trail, Riparian Habitat, Mountain Habitat, Grasslands Habitat and an underground Earth Science Center. Because the museum is built among the upland desert with little disturbance, there is an abundance of free-roaming wildlife that the visitor may encounter. Nowhere else can visitors have close observation of mountain lion, ocelot, coyote, javelina, Mexican gray wolf, river otter, beaver, thick-billed parrot, desert pupfish, Sonora

SKY ISLANDS ■ Arizona-Sonora Desert Museum

Premier ★ SITE ★

chub, bonytail chub, razorback sucker, Gila topminnow, Colorado River pikeminnow, Apache trout and many other species. In the Hummingbird Aviary visitors can see up to eight species of hummingbirds, which regularly hatch and raise young in the enclosure. Birding on the museum grounds is outstanding, with many species acclimated to people and easy to approach. Common species include the Gila woodpecker, Costa's hummingbird, cactus wren, curve-billed thrasher, verdin and white-winged dove.

Trails

The Museum has a mix of paved and flat dirt trails. The paved trails are universally accessible and wheelchairs are available to rent. The Desert Loop Trail, a half-mile long loop through natural desert, features large enclosures where visitors have opportunities to see animals in natural conditions.

Site Notes	Fee site.
Size	30 acres (developed); 70 acres (undeveloped)
Directions	From Tucson, go west on Speedway Boulevard over Gates Pass to Kinney Road. Go right on Kinney Road; follow signs to Desert Museum.
Nearest Town	Tucson
Ownership	Arizona-Sonora Desert Museum Board of Trustees
Contact	520-883-2702 www.desertmuseum.org/
Features	restrooms, trash cans, trails, lookouts, interpretive signs, brochure/species list, visitor center, drinking water, bus/motorhome access, boat ramps, parking, photo blinds

Desert Pupfish

PHOTO BY BRUCE D. TAUBERT

SKY ISLANDS ■ *Arizona-Sonora Desert Museum*

Pyrrhuloxia

PHOTO BY E. J. PEIKER

Gray Wolves

PHOTO BY ANDREA VATNE

SKY ISLANDS ■ *Arizona-Sonora Desert Museum*

Premier
★ SITE ★

PHOTO BY BRUCE D. TAUBERT

Acorn Woodpecker   PHOTO BY BRUCE D. TAUBERT

Description

The Chiricahua Mountain Range is an inactive volcanic range 20 miles wide and 40 miles long. At the northern end of the range is an extraordinary area of striking geological features and enormous biodiversity. Tucked deep into these steep, forested valleys and beneath the craggy peaks are the remains of violent geological activity that continued for many millions of years—the pinnacles, columns, spires and balanced rocks of Chiricahua National Monument. The Apaches called this place "The Land of Standing-Up Rocks," a fitting name for an extraordinary rock wonderland. Early pioneers in the late 1800s sensed the unique beauty of the rock formations in the area. Today, the monument is a mecca for hikers and birders and represents one of the premier areas for biological diversity in the northern hemisphere.

There are approximately 12,000 acres of wild, rugged terrain within which both rock formations and a great ecological diversity are protected. The monument exhibits a unique diversity of plants, including ponderosa pine, Rocky Mountain maple, soap tree yucca, numerous species of oak, Douglas and white fir, cane cholla and prickly pear cactus.

SKY ISLANDS ■ *Chiricahua National Monument*

Premier
★ SITE ★

Wildlife to Watch

There are at least 71 species of mammals, 46 species of reptiles, 8 amphibians, 171 species of birds and uncounted numbers of insects that regularly occur on Chiricahua National Monument. Species like the western box turtle and the cactus wren utilize the grasslands and desert scrub, while the northern goshawk and Mexican spotted owl live in the nearby old-growth ponderosa pine forest. The rock rattlesnake prefers a more specialized habitat, such as rocky slopes and gravelly drainages. The unique geological formations of the monument provide the vertical cliffs that falcons, turkey vulture and white-throated swift need for nesting, while underground faults allow water to spring up in some areas, creating small wetlands for the tiger salamander.

Mammals such as black bear, mountain lion, white-tailed and mule deer, ringtail and bats are common. Several species, such as the coatimundi, Mexican fox squirrel and northern pygmy mouse have limited range in the United States, but are a fairly common sight here. Some of Arizona's most recent jaguar sightings have occurred in the mountains nearby.

The monument's habitats and southern location bring a variety of Mexican bird species across the border, such as the elegant trogon, whiskered screech-owl, Arizona woodpecker and the magnificent hummingbird. In fact, 13 species of hummingbirds are known to occur in the Chiricahua Mountains, and many of these can be found on the monument. Common birds in the area include Mexican jay, black-headed grosbeak, acorn woodpecker, yellow-eyed junco, painted redstart, Grace's warbler and spotted towhee.

Audubon
IMPORTANT
BIRD AREAS

Trails

Chiricahua National Monument features 17 miles of maintained trails of varying degrees of difficulty. The Echo Canyon Trail (3½ miles) and the Heart of Rocks Trail offer spectacular views of balanced rocks, spires and pinnacles. A winding 8-mile scenic drive climbs steadily from the entrance, past the visitor center to Massai Point (elevation 6,870 feet) where several trails branch off, descending into canyons and towards the main rock formations, which are not visible from the road. This is a sloping cliff face, weathered into many rocky columns.

Site Notes Fees site. Dogs are not permitted on trails. Monument offers free hikers' shuttle that leaves the Visitor Center every day at 8:30 a.m. Monument staff drives you to the upper canyon trailheads so you may hike back down the canyon. Seating is very limited.

Size 12,984 acres

Directions Located 120 miles east of Tucson. Take I-10 at Willcox and follow S.R. 186 for 36 miles to park.

Nearest Town Willcox

Ownership National Park Service

Contact 520-824-3560
www.nps.gov/chir/

Features universally accessible trail, restrooms, trash cans, trails, overlooks, lookouts, interpretive signs, brochure/species list, visitor center, museum, drinking water, bus/motorhome access, parking, historic building, campground, picnic area

Yellow-eyed Junco   *PHOTO BY E. J. PEIKER*

Black Bear   *PHOTO BY DON JONES*

Premier
★ SITE ★

PHOTO BY WILLIAM RADKE

A secret garden within an active military base

White-tailed Deer

PHOTO BY DON JONES

Description

One of Arizona's largest military installations, Fort Huachuca was established in 1877 and continues as an active military post. The fort was the headquarters of the 4th Cavalry patrols that pursued Geronimo and his band of Chiricahua Apache and ultimately brought about their surrender in 1886. Fort Huachuca also served as home of the famous buffalo soldiers who, among other exploits, chased Pancho Villa in 1916 following attacks on Columbus, New Mexico. Today, Fort Huachuca is an important military intelligence and communications center, and the expansive installation helps manage and protect important biological diversity on and adjacent to the Huachuca Mountains. Two museums and an annex trace the fort's colorful history. Located within Fort Huachuca, Garden Canyon is sometimes called the most beautiful canyon in the Huachuca Mountains, and this scenic area contains some of the most diverse plant and animal life in the mountain range. This prominent desert landscape is bordered in several areas by creeks, ponds, forests and waterfalls, with a wide variety of wildflowers, mammals, birds, reptiles, amphibians and insects.

Wildlife to Watch

This portion of the Huachuca Mountains and San Pedro River Valley offers good opportunities to see white-tailed deer, pronghorn, javelina, coatimundi, black bear and other mammals. Grasslands are prime habitat for Cassin's and Botteri's sparrows, which are best located while they are singing during July and August. Garden Canyon and its associated side canyons are excellent places to observe the Montezuma quail, Gould's turkey, acorn woodpecker, Mexican jay, elegant trogon, sulphur-bellied and buff-breasted flycatchers, painted redstart

SKY ISLANDS ■ *Fort Huachuca-Garden Canyon*

and red-faced and Grace's warblers. There is also a chance of seeing Mexican spotted owls. Common reptiles include the Yarrow's and Clark's spiny lizards, desert grassland whiptail, Sonoran spotted whiptail, Sonoran whipsnake, Sonoran mountain kingsnake, rock rattlesnake and black-tailed rattlesnake. Wetlands on the fort support the Ramsey Canyon leopard frog. The fort provides varied habitats for a tremendous diversity of land snails, dragonflies and other insects, including many endemic species. Garden Canyon is legendary among butterfly enthusiasts because of its biodiversity.

Audubon
IMPORTANT
BIRD AREAS

Trails

A single-lane dirt road takes you to the top of Garden Canyon, where a short walk and a climb up boardwalk steps leads to a good view of prehistoric rock paintings. The Upper Picnic Area in Garden Canyon provides excellent birding, and trailheads to other canyon areas are found here. The rough, steep Scheelite Canyon Trail begins about $7/10$ mile past the Upper Picnic Area and the steep, but more gentle Sawmill Canyon Trail at the end of Garden Canyon Road continues to climb through classic pine-oak woodland. The road to Garden Canyon is closed occasionally because of military maneuvers and other canyons on the fort, including Huachuca and Blacktail, also offer excellent wildlife viewing opportunities.

Site Notes Fort Huachuca has traditionally been open to the public, but be aware that security concerns can suddenly change and tighten access. Civilian visitors who are U.S. citizens must be prepared to provide photo identification, vehicle registration and/or car rental contract, and proof of insurance. Foreign nationals are allowed to visit only in the company of a U.S. citizen with a military identification card. Additionally, all or parts of the post may be closed to civilians for indefinite periods of time for reasons of public safety and/or national security. All visitors are subject to random inspections by military police.

Size 73,000 acres

Directions From Sierra Vista go west through post main gate, then follow road southwest to Garden Canyon.

Nearest Town Sierra Vista

Ownership Department of Defense, U.S. Army

Contact huachuca-www.army.mil/sites/local/

Features restrooms, trash cans, trails, lookouts, interpretive signs, brochure/species list, visitor center, drinking water, bus/motorhome access, parking

Premier
★ SITE ★

Gould's Turkey

PHOTO BY JOE AND MARISA CERRETA

Sonoran Mountain Kingsnake

PHOTO BY RANDY BABB

Premier
★ SITE ★

PHOTO BY ARIZONA STATE PARKS

Gila Monster

PHOTO BY THOMAS C. BRENNAN

Description

Patagonia Lake State Park, one of the state's premier year round birding spots, is an outstanding example of riparian woodland habitat, dominated by giant Fremont cottonwood, willow, velvet ash and Arizona walnut trees. Extensive mesquite bosques are found in lowland areas at the upper end of the lake. The centerpiece of the park is the 250-acre Patagonia Lake, which provides rare open water habitat that attracts a tremendous variety of wildlife, particularly waterbirds. Visitors come from all over to see southeast Arizona specialty bird species. Riparian habitat is concentrated on the northeast end of the lake, where Sonoita Creek enters. The creek exits the lake to the southwest below the dam providing perennial waters and riparian habitat through the Sonoita Creek State Natural Area. Designated in 1994 as Arizona's first major state natural area, Sonoita Creek State Natural Area provides an important wildlife viewing site, while preserving a unique riparian area.

Wildlife to Watch

Birds of prey include osprey, common black-hawk, gray hawk and zone-tailed hawk; specialty birds include elegant trogon (winter), yellow-billed cuckoo, green kingfisher, broad-billed hummingbird, black-capped gnatcatchers, crissal thrasher, Lucy's warbler, Bell's vireo, varied bunting, summer tanager, hooded oriole and many species of flycatcher, such as vermilion flycatcher and northern beardless-tyrannulet. Wetland birds include Virginia rail, sora, neotropic cormorant, green heron and various species of grebes and ducks. Great blue herons nest in the giant cottonwood trees on the east end of the park. Mammals include white-tailed deer, ringtail, coatimundi, javelina, mountain lion, bobcat and gray fox; lesser long-nosed bats are present but

SKY ISLANDS ■ *Patagonia Lake State Park/Sonoita Creek State Natural Area*

Premier
★ SITE ★

difficult to see. Reptiles include Gila monster, western diamond-backed rattlesnake, green ratsnake, coachwhip and kingsnake. Gila topminnow are found at Coal Mine Spring in the north end of the Natural Area.

Audubon
IMPORTANT
BIRD AREAS

Trails

A 1½-mile trail is open with more trails planned. Site includes self-guided trails with displays.

Site Notes	Fee site. The park offers a variety of guided nature tours. Check website for schedule and availability. Park closures can occur during peak summer visitor months. The park is extremely busy on weekends and holidays and in summer months; please call in advance to determine if closures are in effect.
Size	250 surface acres (lake); 10,546 acres (park and natural area)
Directions	Take I-10 east to Hwy. 83 and go south to Hwy. 82. Take Hwy. 82 7 miles south of Patagonia.
Nearest Town	Patagonia
Ownership	Arizona State Parks
Contact	520-287-6965 www.azstateparks.com/Parks/parkhtml/patagonia.html
Features	restrooms, camp store, trails, visitor center, drinking water, bus/motorhome access, boat ramps, parking, campground, dump station, showers

Broad-billed Hummingbird

PHOTO BY CHARLES W. MELTON

Northern Beardless-Tyrannulet

PHOTO BY BRIAN E. SMALL

Premier
★ SITE ★

PHOTO BY GEORGE ANDREJKO

Pima Orange-tip Butterfly

PHOTO BY WILLIAM RADKE

Description

The San Pedro River enters Arizona from Sonora, Mexico, flows north between the Huachuca and Mule Mountain ranges, and joins the Gila River 100 miles downstream. Along its banks, this riparian area provides habitat for over 375 species of birds. Vegetation along the river corridor includes Fremont cottonwoods, Goodding willow, and other riparian trees and shrubs with adjacent mesquite bosques and dense stands of sacaton grass. Upland areas are Chihuahuan Desert scrub.

The National Conservation Area features many significant archeological and historic sites, including Spanish fortress remains, early Clovis nomadic hunting sites, a mammoth-kill site, historic "ghost towns," and petroglyphs.

Wildlife to Watch

While primarily known for birding, the area has a high diversity of mammal life as well, although many are nocturnal. Mammals include white-tailed and mule deer, javelina, desert cottontail and black-tailed jackrabbit as well as many species of bats and rodents. More than 250 species of butterflies representing five families can be found; in the early fall, hundreds of thousands of butterflies are attracted to wildflowers in bloom. Amphibians such as Mexican spadefoot and red-spotted toad breed in backwaters and ephemeral pools along the river. Clark's spiny lizard is commonly seen on the towering cottonwoods, just one of the many lizard species found in the area. Western hog-nosed snake, gopher snake, coachwhip and western diamond-backed and Mohave rattlesnakes are also found in the area.

Recognized internationally as a premier birding site, this area attracts thousands of birders each year. Over 100 species of breeding birds and over 250 species of migratory and wintering birds occur in this area, representing roughly half the number of known breeding species in North America. Wintering sparrows include vesper, Brewer's, white-crowned, swamp and Lincoln's. Species of birds of prey including the gray, Swainson's, zone-tailed and Cooper's hawks, common black-hawk, northern harrier, elf and western screech-owls can be found here. Other species include the green kingfisher, northern beardless-tyrannulet, yellow-breasted chat, vermilion flycatcher, Say's and black phoebes, blue grosbeak, summer tanager, Cassin's kingbird and yellow-billed cuckoo.

Audubon
IMPORTANT
BIRD AREAS

Trails

The San Pedro Trail parallels the river though most of the conservation area. Two trail sections can be accessed from the San Pedro House (headquarters). The San Rafael del Valle section heads south to Hereford Road (8 miles). The Clanton section begins just north of Hwy. 90 and goes north, past the ruins of the Clanton Ranch (3 miles) to Escapule Rd. (3⅗ miles). An interpretive loop trail begins at the San Pedro House and passes several historic and cultural sites. Be aware of flooding during monsoons.

Site Notes Park at any access point and walk up or down the river for best viewing. Rattlesnakes are common throughout the area. Warm weather visitors should take appropriate precautions to avoid rattlesnakes when hiking or recreating in the NCA and adjacent areas. Though snake encounters are not uncommon, bites from these animals are rare.

Size 60,000 acres

Directions Travel seven miles east of Sierra Vista on SR 90.

Nearest Town Sierra Vista

Ownership Bureau of Land Management

Contact 520-439-6400
www.blm.gov/az/nca/spnca/spnca-info.htm

Features restrooms, trash cans, trails, overlooks, interpretive signs, brochure/species list, visitor center, drinking water, bus/motorhome access, parking

Premier ★ SITE ★

Gray Hawk

PHOTO BY BRIAN E. SMALL

Mexican Spadefoot

PHOTO BY RANDY BABB

Premier
★ SITE ★

PHOTO BY BRUCE D. TAUBERT

Sandhill Crane

PHOTO BY TOM WHETTEN

Description

The Whitewater Draw Wildlife Area, formerly a cattle ranch, was purchased in 1997 and is now managed to enhance wetland habitats and provide waterfowl habitat, management for plains leopard frogs, and wildlife viewing. Available water is managed to provide marshland, mudflats and open water areas. Viewing opportunities are enhanced by viewing decks, an interpretive trail, viewing scopes and an educational kiosk. Several ponds surrounded by native vegetation provide habitat that has become rare in southeast Arizona. Native grasslands, with intermittently flooded wetlands surrounded by agricultural fields, provide shelter and feeding opportunities for sandhill cranes and a wide variety of other birds, amphibians and reptiles.

Wildlife to Watch

The number of wintering sandhill cranes has increased dramatically since the 1950s, and over 30,000 sandhill cranes may be present in winter, making this the premier crane viewing site in Arizona. The number of waterbirds wintering here has also increased in recent years, and when ample water is present, thousands of ducks and other waterbirds are usually present all winter. This is a great place to see avocets, stilts and yellowlegs. Wetland birds include a wide variety of ducks, geese, herons, egrets and migrating shorebirds, gulls and terns. The small stand of riparian woodland attracts many migratory birds including warblers, vireos, flycatchers, orioles, tanagers, grosbeaks, buntings and sparrows. You may see mourning dove, white-winged dove, Gambel's quail and scaled quail. Several species of sparrows can be found, including

SKY ISLANDS ■ *Whitewater Draw Wildlife Area*

Premier
★ SITE ★

147

lark, vesper, white-crowned, Lincoln's and Cassin's. Members of the flycatcher family including vermilion flycatcher, Say's phoebe and black phoebe are common here. Common yellowthroat and marsh wren are easy to find in wetland areas. During winter months look for mountain plover and longspur adjacent to the site in cut alfalfa or barren fields along Davis Road. This site and the surrounding area is the best place to see wintering birds of prey, including golden eagle, prairie and peregrine falcons, northern harrier, Cooper's hawk, American kestrel, merlin, ferruginous hawk, red-tailed hawk and occasionally rough-legged hawk. Mammals include javelina, mule deer, black-tailed jackrabbit and desert cottontail. Whitewater Draw also features the healthiest and most stable of plains leopard frog populations in the state. This frog is one of the most narrowly distributed of all Arizona leopard frogs. A variety of other amphibians live around and breed in the draw including green toad, Great Plains toad, Mexican spadefoot and Sonoran Desert toad. Some of the more common reptiles of the area include western hog-nosed snake, gopher snake, nightsnake, desert kingsnake, common side-blotched lizard, Texas horned lizard and southwestern fence lizard. One of Arizona's more unique invertebrates, the whip-scorpion or vinegaroon, can be commonly viewed in this area, particularly after sunset on paved roadways.

Trails

Short trails are adjacent to parking areas.

Site Notes	During wet weather, dirt roads can become slick with mud; use extreme caution.
Size	1,500 acres
Directions	From U.S. Hwy. 191 at McNeal, drive west on Davis Road for 3 miles to Coffman Road. Turn south on Coffman Road and follow the signs for 2 miles; turn west into parking area and trailhead.
Nearest Town	McNeal
Ownership	Arizona Game and Fish Department
Contact	520-642-3763 www.azgfd.gov/outdoor_recreation/wildlife_area_ whitewater.shtml
Features	restrooms, trash cans, trails, viewing platforms with binoculars, interpretive signs, bus/motorhome access, parking

Vesper Sparrow

PHOTO BY BRUCE D. TAUBERT

Plains Leopard Frog

PHOTO BY THOMAS C. BRENNAN

SKY ISLANDS ■ *Bonita Creek/Gila Box Riparian National Conservation Area*

Bonita Creek/Gila Box Riparian National Conservation Area

PHOTO BY WILLIAM RADKE

Description

One of only two Riparian National Conservation Areas (RNCA) in the country, Gila Box is a unique desert oasis with four perennial waterways: the Gila and San Francisco Rivers and Bonita and Eagle Creeks. The area consists of patchy mesquite woodlands, mature cottonwood trees and buff-colored cliffs. The historic Serna Cabin is located near the confluence of Bonita Creek and the Gila River. Other pioneer cabins, as well as prehistoric Native American ruins, are located throughout Gila Box.

Wildlife to Watch

Bonita Creek has the easiest access and provides a clifftop wildlife-viewing platform. In addition to more than 150 bird species, there are opportunities to view bighorn sheep, beaver, javelina and mule deer. Birders can see canyon wren, common black-hawk and ladder-backed woodpecker.

Numerous beaver dams are found along Bonita Creek; five native fish species inhabit the crystal-clear waters of the creek.

Wildlife viewing is good year-round. Birding is best during spring and fall migration and the summer nesting season. There is distant viewing of bighorn sheep along the canyon cliffs in the upper canyon and along the Gila River. Look for javelina and Coues white-tailed deer along roads.

Great
▲ SITE ▲

Trails

A short, paved trail leads from a parking area to a wildlife-viewing platform; sidewalk is wheelchair accessible but has a gentle slope. Safford-Morenci Trail is 21 miles long from Clifton area to Safford area but can be accessed from a road near Bonita Creek and Midnight Canyon; moderate hike. Primitive roads along Bonita Creek also provide hiking access.

Size 500 acres (Bonita Creek); 22,000 acres (Gila Box RNCA)

Directions From Safford travel approximately 5 miles east on U.S. Hwy. 70 to the town of Solomon and turn left onto Sanchez Road. From there travel north and cross the bridge at the Gila River. Drive 7 miles to the Bonita Creek and Gila Box RNCA sign and turn left onto that dirt road. Travel approximately 2½ miles to the west entry sign of the Gila Box RNCA and continue following signs another 5 miles to Bonita Creek. At the fork, go right to access lower Bonita Creek and the Riverview Campground. The road to the left provides access to the middle and upper stretches of the creek.

Nearest Town Safford and Clifton

Ownership Bureau of Land Management

Contact 928-348-4400
www.blm.gov/az/nca/gila_box/gila.htm

Features restrooms, trash cans, trails, lookouts, interpretive signs, brochure/bird species list, drinking water, parking

Ladder-backed Woodpecker   PHOTO BY BRIAN E. SMALL

Great
▲ SITE ▲

Buenos Aires National Wildlife Refuge

PHOTO BY STEVE HILLEBRAND/USFWS

Description

A landscape of long, sweeping vistas of rippling grasslands flanked by mountains and their everchanging colors and shadows mark the Buenos Aires National Wildlife Refuge in the Altar Valley. Majestic Baboquivari Peak, an ancient volcano that is sacred to the Tohono O'odham Nation, dominates the western mountains edging the refuge. This is one of the best places in Arizona to see open grassland and natural landscapes with minimal marks of human activity. The refuge was established to provide habitat for the endangered masked bobwhite.

There are three refuge units with different habitat types. Most of the area is semi-desert grassland; on the east end are several riparian areas, including Arivaca Cienega and Arivaca Creek. On the west end is Brown Canyon where a sycamore-lined stream flows through oak woodlands.

Wildlife to Watch

The only U.S. refuge where four species of quail are found, including masked, bobwhite, Gambel's, scaled and Montezuma quail.

Birding is good year-round, with abundance and diversity highest in spring and summer. Birds of prey include golden eagle, prairie falcon, crested caracara, Swainson's hawk, western screech-owl and long-eared owl. Wintering sparrows include lark, vesper, white-crowned, chipping and Brewer's, and during the summer monsoon period, the various grasslands are filled with the songs of

Botteri's, Cassin's, rufous-winged, rufous-crowned, lark and grasshopper sparrows. Large flocks of lark buntings also winter on the refuge. Birders come to Brown Canyon to seek out the Montezuma quail, black-capped gnatcatcher, sulphur-bellied flycatcher and a variety of hummingbirds. Many riparian species are at some of the northernmost extension of their subtropical range, such as the gray hawk, buff-colored nightjar, rose-throated becard, tropical and thick-billed kingbirds and green kingfisher.

Mule deer and pronghorn are best seen in the headquarters section along the entrance road. Other species unique to North American prairies are found here, including antelope jackrabbit, loggerhead shrike and Great Plains narrow-mouthed toad.

Audubon
IMPORTANT
BIRD AREAS

Trails

There are four trails ranging from 1¼ to 5 miles in length, as well as a 10-mile self-guided auto tour loop.

Arch Trail in Brown Canyon, accessible by guided hike only, is a 4½-mile round-trip easy walk. It follows a sycamore-lined stream to a 47-foot high natural rock arch.

Site Notes	Limited public access—check access prior to visit. Brown Canyon visits are by guided walks and workshops only and require reservations.
Size	117,342 acres
Directions	From Tucson, drive 15 miles west on Hwy. 86 to Three Points (Robles Junction), then 38 miles south on Hwy. 286 to milepost 7½.
Nearest Town	Arivaca
Ownership	U.S. Fish and Wildlife Service
Contact	520-823-4251 www.fws.gov/southwest/refuges/arizona/buenosaires/index.html
Features	restrooms, trash cans, trails, brochure/ species list, drinking water, parking, campgrounds, observation decks, telescopes

SKY ISLANDS ■ *Buenos Aires National Wildlife Refuge*

Great
▲ SITE ▲

68

Catalina State Park

Wildlife, birds and petroglyphs, all close to Tucson

Catalina State Park

PHOTO BY ARIZONA STATE PARKS

Description

This high desert park at 2,650 feet elevation north of Tucson features a wide array of desert plants and animals as well as archaeological sites. The northwest face of the Santa Catalina Mountains forms the backdrop for the scenic park with its foothills, canyons and streams. Plants include mesquite, paloverde and acacia trees, crucifixion thorn, ocotillo, cholla, prickly pear and saguaro cactus. Desert willow, Arizona sycamore, Arizona ash and native walnut grow along the washes.

Wildlife to Watch

More than 150 species of birds have been documented in the park, including red-tailed and Harris's hawks, elf owl, Gambel's quail, cactus wren, Lucy's warbler, rufous-winged and rufous-crowned sparrows, pyrrhuloxia, broad-billed and Costa's hummingbirds, northern beardless-tyrannulet, gilded flicker and Gila woodpecker. Collared, desert spiny, and canyon spotted and tiger whiptail lizards are easily seen in the warmer months. A variety of snakes may be encountered in the park, including coachwhip, gopher snake, western patch-nosed snake and western diamond-backed rattlesnake. Black-tailed jackrabbit and desert cottontail, mule and white-tailed deer, javelina, coyote and ground squirrel are frequently seen. Mountain lion and black bear have been observed.

Trails

There are eight trails varying in length and difficulty. The Romero Ruin Interpretive Trail (¾ mile) meanders through the ruins of a prehistoric Hohokam village site that is over 1,000 years old. The one-mile Nature Trail offers beautiful vistas and interpretive signs. A one-mile Birding Trail with interpretive signs offers hikers a chance to see some of the park's 170+ species of birds. Trailheads in the park connect to longer, more strenuous hikes that connect with other Coronado National Forest trails.

Site Notes	Fee site.
Size	10,218 acres
Directions	Located 9 miles north of Tucson on State Hwy. 77 (Oracle Road) at mile marker 81.
Nearest Town	Tucson
Ownership	Arizona State Park
Contact	520-628-5798 www.azstateparks.com/Parks/parkhtml/catalina.html
Features	restrooms, trash cans, trails, lookouts, interpretive signs, brochure/species list, visitor center, drinking water, bus/motorhome access, campground, picnic area, parking, equestrian center for off-loading or camping with horses

Harris's Hawk

PHOTO BY BRUCE D. TAUBERT

69

Cave Creek Canyon

Unforgettable scenery and some of the richest wildlife diversity in the United States

Cave Creek Canyon

PHOTO BY WILLIAM RADKE

Description

While out of the way, this site is well worth the effort for avid birders and wildlife watchers. Cave Creek Canyon has some of the richest diversity of wildlife in the United States. The approach from the east through Portal provides striking views of the most scenic, breathtaking canyon in southeastern Arizona. This area is internationally known for its hundreds of bird species due to the influences of the Chihuahuan Desert, subtropical habitats of Mexico and mountain habitats of North America. In Cave Creek you'll find spectacular cliffs, caves and peaks, lush riparian forest, world class birding, unique wildlife and recreational amenities. The South Fork Zoological Botanical Area is set aside for wildlife study and viewing, and the Cave Creek Visitor Center provides interpretive information.

Wildlife to Watch

This is the best location in the U.S. to find elegant trogons and to hear a good variety of owls and nightjars. Birds include the Arizona woodpecker, Mexican jay, plumbeous, Hutton's and Bell's vireos, summer, hepatic and western tanagers, black-headed grosbeak, bridled titmouse, Scott's and hooded orioles, and Montezuma quail. A wide range of warblers, such as Grace's, yellow, Lucy's, Virginia's and black-throated gray warblers, and painted redstart, can be seen, as well as hummingbirds such as broad-billed, blue-throated, Lucifer, magnificent, violet-crowned, black-chinned, broad-tailed and rufous humming-birds. Various flycatchers can be seen, including brown-crested, dusky-capped, ash-throated and sulphur-bellied flycatchers. The site also has an impressive variety of owls, including elf, whiskered screech, western screech, northern (mountain) pygmy, flammulated and Mexican spotted owls.

Mammals include white-tailed deer, Mexican fox squirrel, javelina, coatimundi, hooded, spotted, hog-nosed and striped skunks, and numerous species of bats. Reptiles include Clark's and Yarrow's spiny lizards, black-tailed rattlesnake, the stunningly patterned rock rattlesnake and Arizona's unique green ratsnake. The site also has a tremendous variety of invertebrates, including many species found nowhere else in the world.

Audubon
IMPORTANT
BIRD AREAS

Trails

The site has several trails with varying lengths and difficulty, including some with small stream crossings. There is a short dirt trail to a scenic vista between Stewart Campground and South Fork Road.

Size	6,000 acres
Directions	From Portal, go west on Forest Road 42 for about 1 mile into the Coronado National Forest. Continue past the visitor center to the camping and parking areas.
Nearest Town	Portal
Ownership	U.S.D.A. Forest Service, Coronado National Forest
Contact	520-364-3468 www.fs.fed.us/r3/coronado/forest/recreation/scenic_drives/cave_cr.shtml
Features	restrooms, trash cans, trails, overlooks, interpretive signs, brochure/species list, visitor center, drinking water, bus/motorhome access, parking, campgrounds, picnic area, many areas have universal accessibility

Blue-throated Hummingbird   PHOTO BY CHARLES W. MELTON

Great
▲ SITE ▲

70

Kartchner Caverns State Park

World-class cave system surrounded by desert grasslands

Kartchner Caverns State Park

PHOTO BY ARIZONA STATE PARKS

Description

This world-class cave system just outside Benson at the base of the Whetstone Mountains was discovered in 1974, established as a state park in 1988, and opened to the public in 1999. Its near-pristine condition is extraordinarily protected, allowing visitors to see spectacular cave formations. Located at 4,600 feet elevation, the park is within desert thornscrub dominated by ocotillo, whitethorn acacia and mesquite.

During the summer months, the caverns' Big Room serves as a nursery roost for over 1,000 female cave myotis bats that migrate to Kartchner Cavern to raise their young. The Big Room is closed when bats are present, usually April to September.

Wildlife to Watch

A variety of bats, including cave myotis and Mexican free-tailed bats (seasonally), ringtail, coatimundi, javelina, white-tailed and mule deer, mountain lion, bobcat and a variety of hummingbirds, such as broad-tailed, broad-billed, Costa's and black-chinned may be seen here. The Hummingbird Garden Walk, located on the southwest side of the Discovery Center, is lush with local vegetation specifically chosen to attract hummingbirds and butterflies. The area also provides habitat for black-throated sparrow, Lucy's warbler, Bell's vireo, blue grosbeak, pyrrhuloxia, phainopepla, and Scott's and Bullock's orioles. Birds of prey include great horned owl and Swainson's and red-tailed hawks. Gopher snake, western diamond-backed rattlesnake, collared lizard, Gila monster, desert tortoise and red-spotted toad are commonly seen reptile and amphibian species.

Trails

The Guindani Trail is 4⅕ miles and ranges from easy to strenuous. It leads to the crest of the Whetstone Mountains, and hikers see sweeping vistas.

The Foothills Loop Trail is a 2½-mile loop, moderate to difficult, which climbs the limestone hill north of the cave and descends into a wash. A short spur trail leads to a scenic mountain viewpoint. This trail has interpretive signage.

Site Notes	Reservations are recommended for cave tours.
Size	717 acres
Directions	Take I-10 east toward Benson, exit 3002. Go south on Hwy. 90 for 9 miles.
Nearest Town	Benson
Ownership	Arizona State Parks
Contact	520-586-4100 www.azstateparks.com/Parks/parkhtml/kartchner.html
Features	restrooms, trash cans, trails, interpretive signs, brochure/species list, visitor center, drinking water, bus/motorhome access, parking, picnic areas, campground

Bullock's Oriole

PHOTO BY BRUCE D. TAUBERT

Great
▲ SITE ▲

71

Leslie Canyon National Wildlife Refuge

Sheltered refuge for native fish, abundant wildlife-viewing opportunities

Leslie Canyon National Wildlife Refuge

PHOTO BY WILLIAM RADKE

Description

The Leslie Canyon National Wildlife Refuge is marked by rough mountainous terrain, dominated by Chihuahuan Desert shrubs and desert grasses. Running through the middle of the refuge is Leslie Creek, with valuable riparian habitat and a rare velvet ash-cottonwood-black willow gallery forest. The refuge was established to protect native fish including the Yaqui chub, Yaqui topminnow and Yaqui longfin dace, and also provides habitat for the rare Huachuca water umbel and other wetland plants.

Wildlife to Watch

Lower visitation rates make this a popular site for wildlife photographers and birders seeking solitude. The refuge is home to over 230 different species of resident and migratory birds. These commonly include yellow-breasted chat, Lucy's warbler, summer tanager, broad-billed and violet-crowned humming-birds, varied bunting, Bell's vireo and black-capped gnatcatcher. There is also a good chance of seeing coatimundi and white-tailed deer, with recently discovered Cockrum's shrews present year-round. Reptiles and amphibians include black-tailed rattlesnake, Sonoran whipsnake, Sonoran spotted whiptail, Madrean alligator lizard and Chiricahua leopard frog.

Trails

There are 1½ miles of trails available to hikers, moderate to difficult. Accommodation for visitors with special access needs by reservation.

SKY ISLANDS ■ Leslie Canyon National Wildlife Refuge

Great
▲ SITE ▲

Site Notes	Areas north of Leslie Canyon Road are open to foot traffic only; areas south of Leslie Canyon Road are closed to public access.
Size	2,765 acres
Directions	Approximately 16 miles north of Douglas and 11 miles southeast of McNeal. From Douglas, drive north on Leslie Canyon Road. From McNeal, drive east on Davis Road. The roadway continues east through the refuge toward Rucker Canyon in the adjacent Chiricahua Mountains.
Nearest Town	Douglas or McNeal
Ownership	U.S. Fish and Wildlife Service
Contact	520-364-2104 www.fws.gov/southwest/refuges/arizona/sanbernardino.html
Features	trails, overlooks, brochure/species list, bus/motorhome access, parking

Lucy's Warbler

PHOTO BY TOM VEZO

Great
▲ SITE ▲

Mexican specialty birds in a sycamore-oak canyon

Santa Rita Mountains

PHOTO BY WILLIAM RADKE

Description

A major drainage in the Santa Rita Mountains, Madera Creek flows northward through Madera Canyon to join the Santa Cruz River. The canyon features scenic views of Mt. Wrightson and the broad Santa Cruz Valley. "Madera" means lumber or wood in Spanish, and this canyon served as a major source of timber for the city of Tucson over a century ago. The canyon is known today for its diverse wildlife and cool relief from the desert heat. Madera Canyon is a popular destination for wildlife watchers and nature lovers who come to see the tremendous variety of birds that live here. April and May are the best months for most species, while July through September are best for hummingbirds.

Wildlife to Watch

This site has over 240 species of birds, which includes a list of 15 species of hummingbirds. The lush riparian habitat provides the perfect breeding grounds for such avian specialties as elegant trogon, painted redstart, broad-billed and magnificent hummingbirds, and elf and whiskered screech-owls. Over 100 species of birds are known to breed in Madera Canyon. Look for Mexican jay, bridled titmouse, acorn and Arizona woodpeckers, sulphur-bellied and dusky-capped flycatchers and various warblers, vireos, tanagers, orioles and grosbeaks. In addition, there are frequent sightings of unique mammals and reptiles including coatimundi, Sonoran mountain kingsnake, mountain skink, Yarrow's spiny lizard and Madrean alligator lizard.

SKY ISLANDS ■ Madera Canyon

Great
▲ SITE ▲

Trails

The Madera Nature Trail is accessible from various locations within the canyon. Portions of the lower reaches of the trail are universally accessible, and along higher reaches the gradient steepens. The Roundup Picnic Area offers good views of Mt. Wrightson, lower Madera Canyon and the Santa Cruz Valley. Contact the Forest Service for current trail conditions and accessibility.

Site Notes Fee site. The road to Madera Canyon is a narrow, curving, two-lane paved road with steep grades in places. In winter, there can be snow or patches of ice on the road in the canyon.

Size 640 acres

Directions From Green Valley on I-19, take exit 63 and drive east past the Continental School. Continue east on Forest Road 62 for 9 miles to the junction of Forest Road 70. Follow Forest Road 70 to Madera Canyon.

Nearest Town Green Valley

Ownership U.S.D.A. Forest Service, Coronado National Forest

Contact 520-281-2296
www.fs.fed.us/r3/coronado/forest/recreation/scenic_drives/mader_cyn.shtml

Features restrooms, trash cans, trails, interpretive signs, brochure/species list, drinking water, bus/motorhome access, parking

Elegant Trogon   *PHOTO BY JIM BURNS*

SKY ISLANDS ■ *Madera Canyon*

Great
▲ SITE ▲

73

Patagonia-Sonoita Creek Preserve

Cottonwood-willow riparian forest with more than 300 bird species

Patagonia-Sonoita Creek Preserve

PHOTO BY GEORGE ANDREJKO

Description

American naturalist Joseph Wood Krutch once said that "No other area in Arizona is more deserving of preservation" than Sonoita Creek. This perennial reach of Sonoita Creek supports a riparian corridor with high biodiversity and was the first preservation project of The Nature Conservancy in Arizona in 1966.

The watershed is mostly undeveloped and the natural processes of flooding are largely intact and highly functional. In this excellent example of a cottonwood-willow riparian forest, some of the trees are over 100 feet tall and over 130 years old. Arizona black walnut, velvet mesquite, velvet ash, canyon hackberry and various willows are found throughout the preserve, along with remnant wetlands or cienagas. Many rare and sensitive plant species are found in the Sonoita Creek watershed, including Huachuca water umbel, Santa Cruz striped agave and the Santa Cruz beehive cactus.

Wildlife to Watch

300 bird species can be observed here. Several unusual, rare, or unique species such as black vulture, gray hawk, green kingfisher, thick-billed kingbird, northern beardless-tyrannulet, violet-crowned hummingbird and rose-throated becard attract birdwatchers. Common birds include vermilion flycatcher, yellow and Lucy's warblers, yellow-breasted chat, Bell's vireo, varied bunting, yellow-billed cuckoo, broad-billed hummingbird and elf owl. Other animals inhabiting the preserve include bobcat, white-tailed deer, javelina, coatimundi,

ringtail, coyote, raccoon, red-spotted toad, Mexican spadefoot, elegant earless lizard, Clark's spiny lizard and black-necked gartersnake. This site is also a great place for viewing butterflies, damselflies and dragonflies.

Patagonia-Sonoita Creek is a perennial stream and one of the very few remaining streams that supports four native fish species, including the Gila topminnow and the longfin dace.

Audubon
IMPORTANT
BIRD AREAS

Trails

Two and one-half miles of dirt trails.

Site Notes	Fee site; closed Mondays and Tuesdays. The Visitor Center has interpretive displays and local information. Guided nature walks are conducted every Saturday morning at 9 a.m., year-round.
Size	1,350 acres
Directions	Take I-10 to Rt. 83 to Sonoita; turn west on Hwy. 82 to Patagonia. Turn west on 4th Avenue, turn south on Pennsylvania, cross the creek and continue about 1 mile to the entrance.
Nearest Town	Patagonia
Ownership	The Nature Conservancy
Contact	520-394-2400 www.nature.org/wherewework/northamerica/states/arizona/pre-serves/art1972.html
Features	restrooms, trash cans, trails, interpretive signs, brochure/species list, visitor center, drinking water, parking

Violet-crowned Hummingbird   PHOTO BY CHARLES W. MELTON

74

Ramsey Canyon Preserve

Hummingbirds galore!

Ramsey Canyon Preserve

PHOTO BY WILLIAM RADKE

Description

The beauty of Ramsey Canyon has attracted people for centuries. The canyon namesake is Gardner Ramsey, an early settler. In the 1880s, Ramsey built a 2½-mile road by hand that started at what is now the preserve headquarters and extended to the Hamburg mine area. Located within the Upper San Pedro River Basin in southeastern Arizona, the canyon is renowned for its outstanding scenic beauty and the diversity of its plant and animal life. This diversity—including such highlights as up to 14 species of hummingbirds—is the result of a unique interplay of geology, biogeography, topography and climate.

A spring-fed stream, northeast orientation and high canyon walls provide Ramsey Canyon with a moist, cool environment unusual in the desert southwest. Water-loving plants such as sycamores, maples, lemon lilies and columbines line the banks of Ramsey Creek, often growing within a few feet of cacti, yucca and agaves. Communities ranging from semi-desert grassland to mixed conifer forest are found within the vicinity of Ramsey Canyon Preserve.

Wildlife to Watch

Ramsey Canyon supports unique southwestern bird species, such as painted redstart, Grace's warbler, greater pewee, bridled titmouse, hepatic tanager, Arizona and acorn woodpeckers, Mexican jay and Gould's turkey. During the summer, bird feeders and flowering plants behind the visitor center regularly attract 8–10 species of hummingbirds, with additional rarities such as berylline,

Great
▲ SITE ▲

white-eared and Lucifer hummingbirds occasionally making an appearance. Mid-July through August is typically the peak period for hummingbird diversity and abundance. The canyon is also home to black bear, white-tailed deer, bobcat, gray fox, Arizona gray squirrel, canyon tree frog, Ramsey Canyon leopard frog, mountain tree frog, Madrean alligator lizard, ridge-nosed rattlesnake, Sonoran mountain kingsnake, Yarrow's spiny lizard and over 100 species of butterflies.

Audubon
IMPORTANT
BIRD AREAS

Trails

The Hamburg Trail parallels Ramsey Creek through the preserve before climbing 500 feet in a half-mile series of steep switchbacks. From the overlook, the trail continues upstream through Miller Peak Wilderness Area where it joins other trails.

Site Notes	Fee site. Hours vary seasonally, call for details. Guided nature walks are conducted March through October, with additional birding and natural history programs for adults and children on a seasonal basis.
Size	380 acres
Directions	From Sierra Vista drive south on Hwy. 92 to Ramsey Canyon Rd. Turn right and drive west toward the mountains until you reach the parking lot for Ramsey Canyon Preserve at the end of the road.
Nearest Town	Sierra Vista
Ownership	The Nature Conservancy
Contact	520-378-2785 www.nature.org/wherewework/northamerica/states/arizona/preserves/art1973.html
Features	restrooms, trash cans, trails, interpretive signs, brochure/species list, visitor center, drinking water, parking, nature center with bookstore, hummingbird observation area

Painted Redstart   PHOTO BY BRIAN E. SMALL

SKY ISLANDS ▪ *Ramsey Canyon Preserve*

Great
▲ SITE ▲

Majestic saguaros attract birds, bats, bees and butterflies

Saguaro National Park

PHOTO BY BRUCE D. TAUBERT

Description

Saguaro National Park consists of two districts: Saguaro West and the much larger Saguaro East. The two areas, separated by the city of Tucson, are about 30 miles apart. Together they preserve 87,114 acres of the life and landscape of the Sonoran Desert, including the park's namesake—the saguaro.

Saguaro West embraces a variety of Sonoran Desert life against the backdrop of the rugged Tucson Mountains.

Saguaro East encompasses an aging saguaro forest at the foot of the majestic Rincon Mountains and an exceptional variety of other desert communities. The park is open daily.

Wildlife to Watch

Saguaro cacti provide their flowers and sweet fruits to hungry desert animals and also provide homes to a variety of birds. The gilded flicker and Gila woodpecker excavate nest cavities inside the saguaro's pulpy flesh. When a woodpecker abandons a cavity, elf or western-screech owls, American kestrels, purple martins, flycatchers and finches may move in. Large birds, like Harris's and red-tailed hawks, also use the saguaro for nesting and hunting platforms, and their stick nests are often constructed among the arms of a large saguaro. In turn, ravens and great horned owls may take over an abandoned hawk nest. Saguaro flowers provide food for a variety of desert birds including white-winged dove, Gila woodpecker, gilded flicker, house finch, curve-billed

Great
▲ SITE ▲

thrasher, cactus wren and hummingbirds. A variety of other species including bees, moths, wasps, butterflies, ants and beetles feed on and pollinate the saguaro flowers. The fruit of the saguaro provides nourishment and necessary water to all these species and more. The fallen fruit feed wood rat, Harris' antelope squirrel, black-tailed jackrabbit, mule deer, javelina, coyote, bobcat, desert tortoise and many other animals. Even after death, the fallen saguaro skeleton provides shelter for a variety of desert insects, arthropods, small mammals and reptiles.

The park provides habitat for a wide variety of other wildlife species, including greater roadrunner, verdin, Say's phoebe, canyon towhee, black-tailed gnatcatcher, Bendire's, curve-billed and crissal thrashers, ash-throated and brown-crested flycatchers, Bell's vireo, rufous-winged and black-throated sparrows, Gila monster, desert spiny lizard, zebra-tailed lizard, western banded gecko, desert tortoise, coachwhip, gopher snake and several species of rattlesnakes.

Trails

There are over 150 miles of hiking trails, ranging from flat and easy strolls in the Sonoran Desert to steep and rugged hikes into the Rincon Mountains.

Site Notes   Vehicles with trailers and RVs over 25 feet are not recommended through Gates Pass and should use the Ina Road exit (248) on I-10, traveling west to Sandario Road, then turning left and heading south, following signs to the park.

Size   87,114 acres

Directions   Saguaro National Park East: From Tucson, take Speedway Boulevard (exit 257 on I-10) east to Freeman Road. Take Freeman Road to Old Spanish Trail. Look for signs to the park entrance.

Saguaro National Park West Visitor Center: From Tucson, take Speedway Boulevard west. At the junction of Camino de Oeste, Speedway Boulevard becomes Gates Pass Road. Continue west on Gates Pass Road to Kinney Road. Take Kinney Road north, following signs to the park.

Nearest Town   Tucson

Ownership   National Park Service

Contact   Saguaro National Park East: 520-733-5153
Saguaro National Park West: 520-733-5158
www.nps.gov/sagu

Features   restrooms, trash cans, trails, lookouts, interpretive signs, visitor center, drinking water, bus/motorhome access, parking

Great
▲ SITE ▲

San Bernardino National Wildlife Refuge

PHOTO BY WILLIAM RADKE

Description

The San Bernardino National Wildlife Refuge, on the U.S.-Mexico border, offers outstanding views east across the San Bernardino Valley. Arid lands contrast with areas of artesian wells and seeps, providing small riparian and forested areas. About one quarter of Arizona's native fish species occurred only in the San Bernardino Valley, and the refuge was established to protect and enhance wetlands for these eight fish species. Partly because of the availability of abundant wetlands in this otherwise dry, Chihuahuan Desert region, the area supports an unusually high diversity of plants and animals. The refuge supports 70 different kinds of grasses and acts as home to over 290 different species of resident and migrating birds. The refuge also serves to protect the San Bernardino Ranch National Historic Landmark. A museum is located here at the fully restored 1884 John Horton Slaughter Ranch.

Wildlife to Watch

Along with the adjacent Leslie Canyon, this is the only public land in Arizona where Yaqui chub, Yaqui topminnow, Yaqui catfish and Yaqui beautiful shiner still exist. Other native fish include the Mexican stoneroller and Yaqui longfin dace. Several species of birds, such as the green kingfisher, gray hawk and tropical kingbird utilize the San Bernardino Valley as some of the northern-most limit of their breeding range. Common birds of the refuge include green heron, Virginia rail, scaled quail, ring-necked duck, Mexican duck (mallard), Gould's turkey, northern beardless-tyrannulet, Bell's vireo, vermilion flycatcher, yellow

Great
▲ SITE ▲

warbler, yellow-breasted chat, blue grosbeak, varied bunting, phainopepla, Botteri's and Cassin's sparrows and Gila woodpecker. Birds of prey include Swainson's and Cooper's hawks, common black-hawk, golden eagle, American kestrel and peregrine falcon. Mammals include mule deer, javelina, mountain lion, raccoon, coyote, bobcat, gray fox, badger and coatimundi. Reptiles and amphibians observed on the refuge include the Sonoran mud turtle, Chiricahua leopard frog, Gila monster, Madrean alligator lizard, Mexican gartersnake and regal horned lizard.

There are at least 76 species of damselflies and dragonflies and 132 species of butterflies on the refuge.

Trails

Refuge roads are available for use as hiking trails to walk-in traffic only. Two primary overlooks accessible on foot provide views of the San Bernardino Valley.

Site Notes	Dirt and gravel surface roads; high clearance vehicles preferred.
Size	2,369 acres
Directions	From Douglas, drive east on 15th Street, which turns into Geronimo Trail Road. Drive 16 miles on gravel surfaced road to refuge entrance at Slaughter Ranch.
Nearest Town	Douglas
Ownership	U.S. Fish and Wildlife Service
Contact	520-364-2104 www.fws.gov/southwest/refuges/arizona/sanbernardino.html
Features	restrooms, trash cans, trails, lookouts, interpretive signs, brochure/species list, visitor center, museum, drinking water, bus/motorhome access, parking, picnic area

Scaled Quail　　PHOTO BY JOE AND MARISA CERRETA

Great
▲ SITE ▲

Santa Catalina Mountains-Mt. Lemmon

A scenic drive from the Sonoran Desert floor to the forests of Mt. Lemmon

Santa Catalina Mountains-Mt. Lemmon

PHOTO BY WILLIAM RADKE

Description

The only paved road that leads to the upper reaches of Mt. Lemmon and the Santa Catalina Range is one of the most scenic highways in the Southwest. This 28-mile (one-way) route provides access to a fascinating land of breathtaking vistas, outlandish rockscapes, cool mountain forests and deep canyons spilling out onto broad deserts. The road starts in the lower Sonoran Desert and climbs to the high coniferous forests. Here, you'll find plants, birds, animals and geology that exhibit some of the most wide-ranging natural diversity to be found in any area of comparable size in the continental United States.

Wildlife to Watch

A wide range of birds can be seen as you travel up this route through varied habitats. At higher elevations, look for greater pewee, yellow-eyed junco, Arizona woodpecker, Steller's jay, plumbeous and Hutton's vireos, hepatic and western tanagers, red-faced warbler, painted redstart, black-headed grosbeak, mountain chickadee, violet-green swallow, pygmy nuthatch, and broad-tailed and magnificent hummingbirds. Mammals include white-tailed deer, black bear, mountain lion, bobcat, ringtail, gray fox, Abert's and red squirrels. Reptiles and amphibians include Sonoran mountain kingsnake, Arizona black rattlesnake, tiger rattlesnake, Sonoran whipsnake and canyon treefrog.

Trails

Dozens of hiking trails offer access to the mountain's backcountry canyons and ridges.

Great
▲ SITE ▲

SKY ISLANDS ■ Santa Catalina Mountains-Mt. Lemmon

Size	28-mile route (one way)
Directions	From northeast Tucson, off Tanque Verde Road, take the Catalina Highway to the forest boundary where it becomes the Hitchcock Highway. Continue on through deserts and canyons past overlooks, picnic areas and campgrounds to the top of the mountain.
Nearest Town	Tucson
Ownership	U.S.D.A. Forest Service, Coronado National Forest
Contact	520-749-8700 www.fs.fed.us/r3/coronado/forest/recreation/scenic_drives/ catalina_hwy.shtml
Features	restrooms, trash cans, trails, overlooks, interpretive signs, brochure/species list, drinking water, bus/motorhome access, parking

Red-faced Warbler

PHOTO BY TOM VEZO

Great
▲ SITE ▲

Sulphur Springs Valley Loop and Willcox Playa Wildlife Area *PHOTO BY GEORGE ANDREJKO*

Description

This 35-mile driving tour through the Sulphur Springs Valley offers access to a variety of habitats, including grassland, desert scrub, playa lakes and farm fields. Birding is best from mid-October through March, when more than 15 species of birds of prey may be found here. The annual Wings over Willcox Birding and Nature Festival takes place in nearby Willcox each January. The focal point of the loop is the 28,000-acre Willcox Playa, located at the north end of the valley. When the playa contains ample water, it provides habitat for tens of thousands of migratory birds.

Wildlife to Watch

Over 20 species of wintering sparrows can be found at this site, including white-crowned, lark, Brewer's, vesper, Lincoln's, savannah, Cassin's, black-throated, grasshopper, song and lark bunting. More than 30,000 sandhill cranes can winter in this valley each year. Visitors from around the world come to witness the early morning liftoff of thousands of cranes from the wildlife area. During winter, it is not uncommon to see over 100 birds of prey and up to 12 species in a day's drive, including ferruginous hawk, northern harrier, prairie falcon, bald and golden eagles, red-tailed hawk and great horned and burrowing owls. In summer, turkey vulture and Swainson's hawk replace the northern birds of prey. Permanent residents, such as greater road-runner, scaled and Gambel's quail, crissal thrasher and pyrrhuloxia can also be seen in the area. During the summer, a unique mallard, the Mexican duck,

Great
▲ SITE ▲

breeds in this area. Mule deer, javelina, coyote and bobcat can be seen. During the monsoons, many reptiles and amphibians can be found on this drive. Most common are the common kingsnake, Mohave rattlesnake, three species of spadefoots, green toad and the unique Arizona striped whiptail.

Trails

At the Willcox Playa Wildlife Area, a 3-mile trail to Crane Lake includes directional signs and interpretive displays. At the Arizona Electric Power Cooperative (AEPCO) Apache Station Wildlife Area along Hwy. 191, a sidewalk leads to spotting scopes that provide views into the distant playa.

Site Notes During wet weather, highway shoulders and dirt side roads can become slick with mud; use extreme caution. Dirt roads within the wildlife area.

Size 35-mile loop; 550-acre wildlife area

Directions Sulphur Springs Valley Loop: From Tucson, take I-10 east to Hwy. 191, then south on Hwy. 191 to junction with Hwy. 181 (Sunizona). Continue south towards Elfrida and take Central Highway south to Double Adobe Road, then east back to Hwy. 191 and north to McNeal.

Willcox Playa Wildlife Area: From Willcox, go east on AZ 186 for 6 miles; turn south on Kansas Settlement Road for 4 miles to the wildlife area.

Apache Station Wildlife Area: Take the I-10 exit 331 south for 8½ miles.

Lake Cochise: Just south of Willcox on Hwy. 186, turn into Twin Lakes Golf Course and follow signs to birding area.

Nearest Town Willcox and Pearce

Ownership Arizona Game and Fish Department, Arizona Department of Transportation, Bureau of Land Management, Department of Defense, Cochise County Highway Department, Arizona Electric Power Cooperative, Sulphur Springs Valley Electrical Co-op

Contact 520-628-5376
www.azgfd.gov

Features restrooms, bus/motorhome access, trash cans, trails, parking

Great
▲ SITE ▲

Swift Trail

Breathtaking drive up Mt. Graham from desert scrub to spruce-fir forests

Swift Trail

PHOTO BY WILLIAM RADKE

Description

Experience the ecological equivalent of driving from Mexico to Canada in one leisurely afternoon on this switchbacking mountain road. The main road offers spectacular views of adjacent valleys as it climbs from 2,900 feet to more than 9,000 feet elevation.

The Swift Trail begins in the desert, where cactus, yucca and mesquite are the prevalent plant species. As the climb begins, the landscape changes from low desert scrub, to oak grassland, to pinyon-juniper woodland, and finally to forests of pine, spruce and fir. The road winds past breathtaking panoramas, lush forests and picturesque mountain meadows. Finally, travelers arrive at the alpine meadows and forests of the 9,000-foot-high ridges of the Pinaleño Range, the highest and most extensive range in all the Sky Islands of south-eastern Arizona. Within these alpine habitats at the end of the Swift Trail is Riggs Flat Lake, found at the highest elevation of any lake in southeastern Arizona. Viewing takes place along the entire length of the road with many pull-outs and overlooks.

Wildlife to Watch

Bird migration periods are excellent times to visit this area to see such warblers as yellow-rumped, Grace's, red-faced, Virginia's, olive, black-throated gray and painted redstart, along with such species as acorn and Arizona woodpeckers, band-tailed pigeon, mountain chickadee, red crossbill, pine siskin, yellow-eyed junco, and red-breasted and pygmy nuthatches. Birds of prey along this route include red-tailed, zone-tailed and Cooper's hawks, and northern goshawk. White-tailed deer and Abert's squirrel are commonly seen, and the unique Mount Graham red squirrel can be seen at the highest elevation areas along the road. Black bear are relatively common throughout. Reptiles include twin-spotted rattlesnake, black-tailed rattlesnake, Sonoran mountain kingsnake and Yarrow's spiny lizard.

Trails

There are many trails with varying lengths and difficulty.

Size	35-mile route, but 85-mile round trip from Safford; allow at least 5 hours
Directions	From Safford, head south on Hwy. 191 for approximately 8 miles. Turn right (southwest) on Hwy. 366 (also known as Swift Trail).
Nearest Town	Safford
Ownership	U.S.D.A. Forest Service, Coronado National Forest
Contact	928-428-4150 www.fs.fed.us/r3/coronado/forest/recreation/scenic_drives/ pinaleno_swift.shtml
Features	restrooms, trash cans, trails, lookouts, interpretive signs, brochure/species list, visitor center, drinking water, bus/motorhome access, parking, boat ramps

Red Crossbill   PHOTO BY BRIAN E. SMALL

SKY ISLANDS ■ *Swift Trail*

Great
▲ SITE ▲

Sycamore Canyon/Goodding Research Natural Area

PHOTO BY WILLIAM RADKE

Description

Five miles south of Ruby Road, rugged Sycamore Canyon leads to the Mexican border. The canyon features steep slopes, rugged cliffs and pinnacles that tower over 200 feet above the canyon floor. The canyon is lined in part by Arizona sycamore trees; oak woodlands in the northern end gradually give way to Sonoran desertscrub with saguaro cactus in the southern portions.

An amazing richness of plant species occurs here, and part of the area has been set aside as the Goodding Research Natural Area. Named after botanist Leslie N. Goodding, the area features several plant populations that are either isolated or occurring at the limits of their geographic ranges.

Wildlife to Watch

Over 130 species of birds inhabit the canyon, including elegant trogon, rose-throated becard, thick-billed kingbird, Arizona woodpecker, painted redstart, varied bunting, whiskered screech-owl, northern (mountain) pygmy owl, dusky-capped flycatcher, northern beardless-tyrannulet, five-striped and rufous-crowned sparrows, Montezuma quail and black vulture. Mammals include white-tailed deer, javelina, coyote, coatimundi and gray fox. Several rare or unusual animals occupy the canyon, such as the Sonora chub, mountain skink, canyon spotted whiptail and Chiricahua leopard frog.

SKY ISLANDS ■ *Sycamore Canyon/Goodding Research Natural Area*

Great
▲ SITE ▲

Ring-necked snake, Sonoran mountain kingsnake and tiny Yaqui black-headed snake are a few of the many snake species inhabiting these mountains and canyons. The rare and unusual brown vinesnake has been seen here along with many other species of tropical reptiles.

Audubon
IMPORTANT
BIRD AREAS

Trails

The Sycamore Canyon trail is five miles long and follows the canyon to the international border. The trail is unmarked and difficult to distinguish, although it follows the general course of the canyon. It is generally flat and gravelly and passes perennial riffles and shallow pools, although cobble and rock hopping is required in some areas. Certain sections also require wading through the creek, which can be deep and muddy.

Site Notes Poison ivy is common along the trail. During the monsoon season (July–September) beware of the flash flooding in this rugged, narrow canyon.

Size 1,000 acres

Directions Take the Pena Blanca Lake/Ruby Road/Hwy. 289 exit (Exit 12) off I-19 and proceed west on Ruby Road. When Ruby Road changes to FR 39 (Pena Blanco Recreation Area) continue for 8½ miles to Sycamore Canyon Road (FR 218). Turn left (south) and proceed a short distance to the parking area.

Nearest Town Nogales

Ownership U.S.D.A. Forest Service, Coronado National Forest

Contact 520-281-2296
www.fs.fed.us/outdoors/
naturewatch/arizona/
botany/sycamore-canyon/
index.shtml

Features trails, parking

Arizona Woodpecker   PHOTO BY TOM VEZO

Great
▲ SITE ▲

Tucson Mountain Park

PHOTO BY BRUCE D. TAUBERT

Description

This is one of the best examples of upper Sonoran Desert in the state. The density of saguaro cacti that cover the hillsides along Gates Pass Road is unique to the area. The geologic formations are visually astounding; the sheltering effects of the rocky outcroppings and wash embankments provide a reliable show of wildflowers following winter and summer rains. There are spectacular views of Avra Valley and the surrounding mountains from the Gates Pass overlook, and petroglyphs are found on some of the canyon walls.

Wildlife to Watch

There are wildlife viewing opportunities from the parking lot trailhead and all along the network of trails. The desert landscape attracts many common Sonoran Desert species such as Gambel's quail, white-winged dove, elf owl, Costa's hummingbird, gilded flicker, Gila and ladder-backed woodpeckers, ash-throated and brown-crested flycatchers, Bell's vireo, black-tailed gnatcatcher, cactus wren, black-throated sparrow and canyon towhee. The rocky outcroppings provide habitat for desert spiny lizard, western patch-nosed snake, black-tailed rattlesnake and tiger rattlesnake. The natural seep in the wash provides an important source of water for mule deer and javelina. Arizona's unique raptor, the Harris's hawk, can be found here.

SKY ISLANDS ■ *Tucson Mountain Park*

Great
▲ SITE ▲

Trails

The park has an extensive trail system to accommodate all capabilities. Most of the roadside turnouts have a trail that leads off into the desert and often connects to the main park trail system.

Site Notes Guided walks with a focus on wildlife viewing are offered on weekends during the months of November–April along the King's Canyon trail that enters Saguaro National Park. Tucson Mountain Park is also home to the Arizona Sonoran Desert Museum.

Size 19,942 acres

Directions From Tucson, travel west on Speedway Boulevard over Gates Pass to the intersection of Kinney Road. Turn north on Kinney Road. Turn right into dirt parking lot just past the entrance to the Arizona-Sonora Desert Museum.

Nearest Town Tucson

Ownership Pima County Natural Resources Parks and Recreation

Contact 520-877-6000
www.pima.gov/pksrec/natres/tucmts/tumtpk.html

Features trails, lookouts, brochure/species list, bus/motorhome access, parking, campground, picnic areas

White-winged Dove

PHOTO BY BRUCE D. TAUBERT

Great
▲ SITE ▲

82

Tumacacori National Historical Park

Spanish colonial mission adjacent to cottonwood-willow forest

Tumacacori National Historical Park

PHOTO BY GEORGE ANDREJKO

Description

The Spanish colonial missions of San Jose de Tumacacori and Los Santos Angeles de Guevavi, established in 1691, are the oldest missions in Arizona. This National Historical Park encompasses the ruins of these and the mission of San Cayetano de Calabazas in the upper Santa Cruz River Valley of southern Arizona.

Tumacacori National Historical Park is uniquely situated at 3,260 feet elevation in the Sonoran Desert, on the banks of the flowing Santa Cruz River. Temperatures in the summer are warm to hot and mild in the winter. These are optimum growing conditions for a variety of desert plants—grasses, trees, shrubs and succulent plants.

Wildlife to Watch

Many bird species are seen at the park due to its proximity to the Santa Cruz River, a short ¼-mile hike from the park center. Nine species of hummingbirds have been seen here, including sightings of violet-crowned and broad-billed hummingbirds. Common resident species observed include curve-billed thrasher, vermilion flycatcher, Abert's towhee and Gila woodpecker, while spring and summer months bring a wide variety of warblers, summer tanager, blue grosbeak, and lazuli, indigo and varied buntings. Many reptile and amphibian species are found on the park's grounds including Clark's spiny lizard, checkered gartersnake and ring-necked snake.

Great
▲ SITE ▲

Trails

The Juan Bautista de Anza National Historic Trail, a long distance National Historic Trail, will run from Nogales to San Francisco, California.

The first section of this trail to be opened to the public in Arizona lies between Tumacácori National Historical Park and Tubac Presidio State Historic Park. From this point, the length of the trail is 4½ miles. If the hiker does not wish to cross the river, it is approximately 1¼ miles from either trailhead to the first river crossing.

Site Notes Fee site. Visits to the Guevavi and Calabazas Missions are available only by reservation during monthly tours guided by the park staff. All visitor services and park operations are based out of the Tumacácori unit.

A variety of interpretive programs are offered, including 40- to 60-minute ranger-guided tours in the winter. Living history programs and interpretive nature walks are also available.

Size 360 acres

Directions Take I-19 south from Tucson 45 miles to exit 29 and follow the signs. The park is 18 miles north of Nogales, AZ, which is on the Mexican border.

Nearest Town Nogales

Ownership National Park Service

Contact 520-398-2341
www.nps.gov/tuma/

Features restrooms, trash cans, trails, lookouts, interpretive signs, brochure/species list, visitor center, drinking water, bus/motorhome access, parking

Abert's Towhee   PHOTO BY BRUCE D. TAUBERT

SKY ISLANDS ■ *Tumacacori National Historical Park*

Great
▲ SITE ▲

Aravaipa Canyon Wilderness

83

Description

Aravaipa is one of Arizona's most scenic canyons, with stunning multicolored cliffs studded with saguaro cactus rising above the canyon. Fern-draped grottoes, seeps and springs line the 19,400-acre canyon. There are numerous archaeological sites, including a cliff dwelling along Turkey Creek.

Wildlife to Watch

Aravaipa is famed as a birder's paradise, with nearly every type of desert songbird and more than 150 species.

The sheer cliffs are good places to look for bighorn sheep. Riparian species include javelina, white-tailed and mule deer, coyote, mountain lion, ringtail and coatimundi. Nearly a dozen bat species flourish in Aravaipa's small caves. Aravaipa Creek is often considered the best native fish habitat in Arizona, the only low-desert creek in the state with an unprecedented seven species of native fish.

Trails

The 11-mile trail follows Aravaipa Creek through Aravaipa Canyon; several side canyons are worth exploring. Overall the trail is easy to moderate in difficulty and requires continual creek crossings.

Site Notes Fee site. Wilderness permit required from BLM. While a hiker can cross from the west end of Aravaipa Canyon Wilderness to the east end by hiking only 11 miles, the entrances are nearly 200 miles apart by road. Canyons are subject to flooding; be aware of weather forecast before entering.

Directions West end: Go 8 miles north of Mammoth, then east on Aravaipa Canyon Road located near Central Arizona College campus, and travel 12 miles to the trailhead.

Contact Bureau of Land Management; 928-348-4400
www.blm.gov/az/sfo/aravaipa/aravaipa.htm

Features West end: restrooms, trails, brochure/species list, parking
East end: restrooms, trails, interpretive signs, brochure/species list, drinking water, parking, campground

Carr Canyon-The Reef

Description

Since 1878, Carr Canyon has been the site of mining activity. The mostly unpaved switchback road leading to the canyon is not for the faint of heart but offers spectacular views of the San Pedro River Valley and a chance to see some of southern Arizona's high country without a long hike. The area has experienced several catastrophic wildfires; today, these areas of disturbance are well on their way to healing.

Wildlife to Watch

Most of the high-elevation bird species of the Sky Islands region can be found here. Look for greater pewee, buff-breasted flycatcher, Arizona and acorn woodpeckers, yellow-eyed junco, Steller's jay, plumbeous and Hutton's vireos, and hepatic and western tanagers. Mammals include black bear, white-tailed deer and raccoon. Reptiles include Slevin's bunch-grass lizard, Yarrow's spiny lizard, ridge-nosed rattlesnake and Sonoran mountain kingsnake.

Audubon
IMPORTANT
BIRD AREAS

Trails

The Reef Townsite Interpretive Loop Trail (#102) begins and ends at the campground (about ½ mile). The trail to Comfort Springs begins off the west end of the Ramsey Vista Campground, drops 200 feet in elevation, and loops through the headwater ravines of Carr Canyon (about ⅗ mile one way).

Directions From Sierra Vista, take Hwy. 92 south for 7 miles, turn west on Carr Canyon Road (FR 368) and continue for 8 miles to the end of the road and the trail access points.

Contact U.S.D.A. Forest Service, Coronado National Forest; 520-378-0311; www.fs.fed.us/r3/coronado/forest/recreation/scenic_drives/carr_cyn.shtml

Features restrooms, trash cans, trails, overlook, interpretive signs, parking, picnic area, campgrounds

Cienega Creek Natural Preserve   85

Description

At the 4,100-acre Cienega Creek Preserve, a perennial creek channel is surrounded by mountains and rocky hills. A section of the creek within the preserve has been designated as a "Unique Water of Arizona." One of the most significant vantage points is the area near the Marsh Station Road Bridge over Cienega Creek.

Wildlife to Watch

The lush riparian vegetative community along the creek accommodates a great number of wildlife species that include mammals, birds, fish, reptiles, amphibians and invertebrates. Visitors should watch for lowland leopard frog, checkered gartersnake, common kingsnake, Gila topminnow, yellow-billed cuckoo, northern beardless-tyrannulet, summer tanager, blue grosbeak, gray and Cooper's hawks and mule deer.

Trails

Audubon
IMPORTANT
BIRD AREAS

There is no designated trail system within the preserve.

Site Notes The preserve is a protected riparian system without designated trails or facilities for visitors. The Arizona Trail System along the edge of the preserve allows equestrian, biking and hiking use. The management plan for Cienega Creek Preserve restricts the number of visitors per day, and permits are required for access.

Directions Take I-10 to Sonoita exit, then take Marsh Station Road east to parking area at the three bridge area.

Contact Pima County; 520-877-6158
www.pima.gov/nrpr/places/parkpgs/1cienega/index.htm

Features no facilities

Other sites

Cluff Ranch Wildlife Area

Description

Cluff Ranch Wildlife Area lies on 800 acres in southeastern Arizona on the north aspect of the Pinaleno Mountains. The landscape varies from low-lying desert hills extending from the mountain slope to generally flat desert plains below. The well-developed riparian woodland habitat is typical of the high-quality vegetative communities once found along the upper Gila River.

Wildlife to Watch

Birds include mourning and white-winged doves, Gambel's quail, greater roadrunner and a variety of migratory and summering birds, such as phainopepla, vermilion flycatcher, summer tanager, Lucy's warbler, hooded oriole and blue grosbeak. Several species of birds of prey, such as Cooper's, red-tailed and gray (recently nesting) hawks, and great horned, elf and western screech-owls all breed here. Visitors may see Clark's spiny and ornate tree lizards, canyon spotted whiptail or round-tailed horned lizard.

Trails

A ½-mile trail begins at the parking lot and includes interpretive signage.

Site Notes During wet weather, highway shoulders and dirt side roads can become slick with mud; use extreme caution.

Directions Take Main Street south from Pima and follow the signs to Cluff Ranch, about 7 miles.

Contact Arizona Game and Fish Department; 928-485-9430 www.azgfd.gov/outdoor_recreation/wildlife_area_cluff.shtml

Features restrooms, trash cans, trail, lookouts, interpretive signs, brochure/species list, visitor center, parking, boat ramp, campgrounds, picnic table

Cochise Stronghold East

87

Description

East Stronghold Canyon provides access into the Dragoon Mountains, one of the twelve "sky islands" of the Coronado National Forest. This rugged 200-acre canyon with large granite boulders was once the home of Cochise, the legendary Apache Chief. There are views of Rockfellow Dome Park to the west, with large granite boulders in the skyline. A self-guided nature trail is adjacent to East Stronghold Campground.

Wildlife to Watch

Look for Mexican jay, dusky-capped flycatcher, bridled and juniper titmouse, canyon and rock wrens, hepatic tanager, black-headed grosbeak, Scott's oriole, rufous-crowned sparrow, black-chinned hummingbird, prairie falcon, white-tailed deer, coatimundi and a variety of butterflies. Clark's spiny lizard, southwestern fence lizard and banded rock and black-tailed rattlesnakes can also be found.

Other sites

Trails

$\frac{1}{10}$ mile of paved, self-guided, cultural resource trail (universally accessible); 1-mile nature trail (loop), moderate difficulty surfaced with natural materials; forest trails about four miles (one way); moderate to difficult.

Directions From I-10 (Exit 331), go south on Hwy. 191, 18 miles to Sunsites; turn west on Ironwood Road and go 10 miles to the site.

Contact U.S.D.A. Forest Service, Coronado National Forest; 520-364-3468; www.fs.fed.us/r3/coronado/forest/recreation/camping/sites/cochise_stronghold.shtml

Features restrooms, trash cans, trails, interpretive signs, drinking water, bus/motorhome access, parking, campground, picnic area

Colossal Cave Mountain Park   88

Description

Spectacular views of the Sonoran Desert greet visitors to this 2,000-acre park with vistas reaching the Santa Rita, Empire, Whetstone and Huachuca Mountains. The vast desert and canyon walls and lush trees line the streambed below. The slopes and ridges are covered by arid succulents such as desert spoons, shindaggers, yuccas and saguaros.

Wildlife to Watch

This site allows exceptional opportunities to view wildlife. The cave is home to a variety of migratory bats, including all three of Arizona's leaf-nosed bats, the California leaf-nosed, Mexican long-tongued and lesser long-nosed bats. Other mammals include mule and white-tailed deer, javelina, bobcat, ringtail, coyote and coatimundi. Birding opportunities are better at the creek and campground within the dense mesquite trees and at the trail that follows the riparian area at La Posta Quemada Ranch. Reptiles include desert tortoise, Gila monster and desert spiny lizard.

Trails

The cave tour route is $\frac{1}{2}$ mile long and takes about 45–50 minutes, with a guide. The trail descends about six and a half stories to view cave formations like stalactites, stalagmites, flowstone, boxwork and helictites. The park has several opportunities for hiking and horseback riding, including a loop trail, connections to the Arizona Trail and an archaeological trail.

Site Notes Fee site. Cave tours are available.

Directions Take I-10 east from Tucson to exit 279 (the Vail exit), turn north and follow the signs for about 7 miles.

Contact Pima County Natural Resources Parks and Recreation; 520-647-7275; www.colossalcave.com

Features restrooms, trash cans, trails, overlooks, interpretive signs, brochure/species list, visitor center, drinking water, bus/motorhome access, campground, parking

SKY ISLANDS ■ Other Sites

Other sites

Coronado National Memorial 89

Description

This 4,750-acre remote corner of the Huachuca Mountains commemorates the expedition of Francisco Vasquez de Coronado in 1549, the first known appearance of Europeans into the United States. Several hiking trails through the wooded foothills of the Huachuca Mountains, excellent views over the river valley, a cave, and an interesting variety of plant and animal life attract visitors.

Wildlife to Watch

White-tailed deer, coatimundi, mountain lion, Montezuma quail, Mexican jay, Arizona woodpecker, dusky-capped flycatcher, white-breasted nuthatch, bridled titmouse, painted redstart, black-headed grosbeak, hepatic tanager, various species of hummingbirds, black-tailed rattlesnake, and Clark's spiny lizard may be encountered here. The secretive barking frog inhabits the rocky canyon slopes of the site and is active only a few weeks of the year.

Audubon
IMPORTANT
BIRD AREAS

Directions Travel south from Sierra Vista on Hwy. 92 to South Coronado Memorial Drive. Follow this road 5 miles to Visitor Center.

Contact National Park Service; 520-366-5515; www.nps.gov/coro/

Features restrooms, trash cans, trails, overlooks, interpretive signs, brochure/species list, visitor center, drinking water, bus/motorhome access, parking, picnic area

Ed Pastor Kino Ecosystem Restoration Project (KERP) 90

Description

The riparian and open water components of this 141-acre site provide invaluable habitat for urban wildlife, as well as an important public education tool. The project restores the habitat of the original Tucson Basin, including riparian, mesquite bosques, upland, creosote, and grassland. Outstanding views of the restored native habitat are available from the path that circles the site.

Wildlife to Watch

Displaced burrowing owls are relocated to KERP, with numerous burrowing owl nesting tunnels. You also may see desert cottontail, black-tailed jackrabbit, red-tailed hawk, red-winged blackbird, Gambel's quail, tiger whiptail, common side-blotched lizard, and a variety of ducks.

Trails

There is a 2⅕-mile loop trail around perimeter of the 141-acre site.

Site Notes The Tucson Audubon Society leads monthly bird walks here on the fourth Saturday of the month.

Directions KERP is north of Ajo Way and west of Country Club Road in Tucson.

Other sites

From Kino Parkway, go east on Ajo Way. Turn left (north) on Forgeus. Follow the signs to the Kino Recreation Center or Sam Lena Park, and park there. KERP is north and west of the park and the recreation center.

From the east, go west on Ajo Way and turn right (north) on Country Club Road. Take the first left into Sam Lena Park. KERP is to the north and west of the park.

Contact Pima County; 520-243-6347; www.pima.gov/ced/CR/KERP.html

Features restrooms, trash cans, trails, drinking water, bus/motorhome access, parking, picnic area

Feliz Paseo Park
91

Description

Feliz Paseo Park features a sensational setting with the Tucson Mountains as a backdrop, diverse native vegetation, deep washes, a wildlife waterhole, and interesting geologic features. The 50-acre site offers wildlife viewing opportunities for people of all abilities, and is close to Tucson on the route to Tucson Mountain Park and the Sonoran Desert Museum.

Wildlife to Watch

There are excellent opportunities to see Gila woodpecker, white-winged dove, Gambel's quail, canyon towhee, cactus wren and other common desert birds. Mule deer, javelina, gopher snake and desert spiny lizard are a few examples of the variety of species.

Trails

The park features universal access trails, with a loop trail and an extensive network of connecting trails with wildlife viewing overlooks throughout the park. Distances and accessibility ratings are posted along all trails, with interpretive and directional signage.

Directions From Tucson take Speedway Boulevard west to Camino Del Oeste. Turn right on Camino Del Oeste; Feliz Paseo Park Entrance will be on the east side of the road north of Speedway Blvd.

Contact Pima County Natural Resources Parks and Recreation; 520-877-6000; www.pima.gov/pksrec/home2/home3.html

Features restrooms, trash cans, universal access trails, lookouts, interpretive signs, brochure/species list, drinking water, bus/motorhome access, parking

Fort Bowie National Historic Site
92

Description

Fort Bowie includes most of historic Apache Pass where the Dos Cabezas Mountains meet the Chiricahua Mountains. These two mountain ranges represent a unique blending of plants and animals from the southern Rocky Mountains and the northern Sierra Madre Mountains.

Wildlife to Watch

Mammals include mountain lion, coatimundi, white-tailed deer, javelina, ringtail and many reptiles, including round-tailed, Texas and greater short-horned lizards, green ratsnake, and banded rock and black-tailed rattlesnakes. Over 150 species of birds nest in the area including scaled and Gambel's quail, Chihuahuan raven, canyon wren, Bell's vireo, black-tailed gnatcatcher, canyon towhee, Lucy's warbler, hooded oriole and Bullock's oriole.

Trails

Loop trail, three miles round trip in mostly open grassland

Directions Located twelve miles south of Bowie, or 116 miles east of Tucson

Contact National Park Service; 520-847-2500 www.nps.gov/fobo

Features restrooms, trash cans, trails, overlook, interpretive signs, brochure/species list, visitor center, drinking water, bus/motorhome access, parking

Las Cienegas National Conservation Area · 93

Description

The Las Cienegas National Conservation Area (NCA) encompasses one of the best grasslands left in southeastern Arizona. This scenic landscape of vast desert grasslands and rolling oak-studded hills connects several "sky island" mountain ranges. This regionally-significant 42,000-acre open space extends south to northern Sonora, Mexico.

Wildlife to Watch

Wildlife species include 60 mammals, 230 birds, 43 reptiles and amphibians and 3 native fish. Large mammals include mule and white-tailed deer, javelina and mountain lion. Small herds of pronghorn are often seen along State Road 82. Several unique species can also be found, including Chiricahua leopard frog, Gila chub, Gila topminnow, lesser long-nosed bat and willow flycatcher.

Trails

There are no developed trails; hiking is possible along primitive roads.

Directions From I-10 east of Tucson, take Exit 281 onto State Road 83. Travel south about 30 miles to the entrance of the NCA, located on the east side of the road. This entrance is located 7 miles north of Sonoita.

Contact Bureau of Land Management; 520-258-7200 www.blm.gov/az/nca/lascienegas/lascieneg.htm

Features restrooms, trash cans, trails, lookouts, interpretive signs, brochure/bird species list, drinking water, parking

Muleshoe Ranch Cooperative Management Area · 94

Description

This remote 49,120-acre area, jointly owned and managed by The Nature Conservancy, Bureau of Land Management and the Forest Service, protects a wide variety of habitats. The plant diversity ranges from saguaro cactus to ponderosa pine forest and contains some of Arizona's best remaining native fish and riparian habitats.

Wildlife to Watch

Six perennial streams provide habitat for five native fish: Gila chub, longfin dace, speckled dace and two species of suckers. The ranch is also home to bighorn sheep, white-tailed deer, black bear and mountain lion. Two hundred bird species can be seen here and include zone-tailed and gray hawks, common black-hawk, broad-billed hummingbird, bridled titmouse and acorn woodpecker. A variety of reptiles and amphibians inhabit the riparian corridor and adjacent desert scrub and woodlands.

Trails

There are 22 miles of trails, of variable levels of difficulty. The Jackson Cabin Road provides access from the ranch headquarters to the BLM Redfield Canyon Wilderness and the USFS Galiuro Wilderness.

Site Notes Guided nature hikes are offered to guests who lodge at the ranch.

Directions Take I-10 east to Willcox, exit 340. After exiting, go south to the first right turn, Bisbee Avenue. Follow Bisbee Avenue to Airport Rd. Turn right on Airport Rd. After about 15 miles, take the right fork at Muleshoe Ranch Road and follow for another 14 miles to the Muleshoe Ranch Headquarters.

Contact The Nature Conservancy; 520-507-5229

Features restrooms, trash cans, trails, lookouts, interpretive signs, brochure/species list, visitor center, drinking water, parking

Oracle State Park
95

Description

This 3,948-acre state park lies in the northern foothills of the Santa Catalina Mountains among an oak grassland and upland mesquite desert scrub landscape. Tours of the historic Kannally Ranch House (National Register of Historic Places), nature education programs for school groups and the general public, and access to a 7-mile section of the Arizona Trail are the major attractions.

Wildlife to Watch

Birds of prey include red-tailed, Cooper's and sharp-shinned hawks, elf and great horned owls. In the winter, you can see several species of sparrows, including black-chinned, black-throated and white-crowned sparrows. Other birds include green-tailed and canyon towhees, loggerhead shrike, bushtit and curve-billed and crissal thrashers. Mammals include white-tailed and mule deer, javelina, mountain lion, bobcat, coyote and gray fox. You can also see a variety of lizards and snakes, including gopher snake, Gila monster, tiger whiptail, and collared and common side-blotched lizards.

Trails

Multiple trails for different hiking abilities. Some loops are less than 1 mile long.

Site Notes Fee site.

Directions From Oracle, follow American Avenue 2⅓ mile to Mt. Lemmon Road. Turn right on Mt. Lemmon and follow it 2⅕ miles to the park entrance.

Other sites

Contact Arizona State Parks; 520-896-2425;
www.azstateparks.com/Parks/parkhtml/oracle.html

Features restrooms, trails, interpretive signs, brochure/species list, drinking water,
bus/motorhome access, parking, photo blinds

Parker Canyon Lake   96

Description

Located in the rolling, evergreen oak woodland hill country and surrounded
by distant mountains, 300-acre Parker Canyon Lake is highly scenic. It
features distant views of the Huachuca Mountains, Patagonia Mountains
and Canelo Hills.

Wildlife to Watch

In winter, the open water attracts bald eagles and a variety of waterfowl.
Osprey and occasional white-faced ibis may be seen feeding at the lake.
Montezuma quail can be seen from the road and the surrounding oak
woodlands are home to Arizona woodpecker, dusky-capped flycatcher,
Hutton's vireo, Mexican jay, bridled titmouse and Scott's oriole. Elegant
earless lizards are common along the shores of the lake and Clark's spiny
lizards inhabit many of the oak and other large trees of the area.

Trails

A five-mile dirt loop trail around the lake is nearly level and easy to follow;
includes trailside benches and interpretive signs.

Directions From Sonoita, drive 30 miles southeast on Hwy. 83 to lake entrance sign.

Contact U.S.D.A. Forest Service, Coronado National Forest;
520-378-0311; www.fs.fed.us/r3/coronado/forest/recreation/lakes/parker_lake.shtml

Features restrooms, trash cans, trails, interpretive signs, drinking water,
bus/motorhome access, boat ramps, parking, campground, convenience store,
boat rental, picnic tables

Roper Lake State Park   97

Description

Roper Lake, at 3,130 feet elevation, is formed by warm-water springs and
surrounded by mesquite, salt cedar and paloverde trees. The lake is a
major stopover and nesting spot for many migrating birds. At the
Dankworth Pond site, follow a self-guided trail. Enjoy an outstanding
view of nearby Mount Graham.

Wildlife to Watch

A wide variety of wetland birds including common merganser, Mexican
duck (mallard), egrets, great blue heron, least bittern and American coot
can be seen. The adjacent trees attract vermilion flycatcher, black phoebe,
Bell's vireo, Lucy's warbler, blue grosbeak, hooded and Bullock's orioles and
pyrrhuloxia. The checkered gartersnake is one of the most commonly seen
of the many reptile species.

Trails

There are five miles of trails throughout the park.

Site Notes Fee site.

Directions Located on U.S. Hwy. 191, 6 miles south of Safford.

Contact Arizona State Parks; 928-428-6760; www.azstateparks.com/Parks/parkhtml/roper.html

Features restrooms, trash cans, trails, overlook, interpretive signs, brochure/species list, visitor center, drinking water, bus/motorhome access, campground, boat ramps, fishing docks, parking, natural hot spring, picnic areas

Roy P. Drachman Agua Caliente Regional Park   98

Description

The 101-acre Agua Caliente Park is named for the perennial warm-water spring that creates a unique desert oasis. There are scenic vistas of the Santa Catalina and Rincon Mountains.

Wildlife to Watch

The palm trees provide a variety of habitats: the fruits provide food for raccoon and Gila woodpecker; the palm skirts provide nesting and roosting sites for hooded oriole, great horned owl and bats. From the shore of the main pond, visitors can view springtime spawning beds of tilapia and largemouth bass. Along the shore, sunny spots may have exotic turtles, such as pond slider and spiny softshell. A visit to the park between October and March will generally provide close views of more than 11 species of ducks attracted to the open waters. Over 150 species of birds have been identified at the site.

Agua Caliente Park is a great location for enjoying the increasingly popular observation of butterflies and dragonflies.

Trails

All trails, wildlife viewing areas and amenities are universally accessible; 1¼ miles of nature trail is paved or hard-packed crushed stone.

Site Notes A wide range of scheduled educational programs are offered at the Historic Rose Cottage. Binoculars and scopes are available for use during naturalist-led activities. The park is free, open daily, and visitation peaks from November to April.

Directions From Tucson, travel east on Tanque Verde Road to Soldiers Trail Road, then north to Roger Road. Turn east on Roger Road to park entrance.

Contact Pima County Natural Resources Parks and Recreation; 520-749-3718; www.pima.gov/pksrec/parkpgs/agua/agua.html

Features restrooms, trash cans, trails, lookouts, interpretive signs, brochure/species list, visitor center, drinking water, bus/motorhome access, parking

SKY ISLANDS ■ *Other Sites*

Other sites

Rustler Park Recreation Area

99

Description

At 8,500 feet, this 30-acre mountain meadow recreation area is nestled in a pine-fir forest. This is one of the few maintained road access sites to upper levels of the Chiricahua Mountains, with breathtaking views that overlook the Sulphur Springs Valley and adjacent landscapes of New Mexico.

Wildlife to Watch

Unique and local nesting forest bird species can be found near campgrounds and along adjacent trails and roadways. This area features the southern-most stand of Engleman spruce, as well as iris and orchids that attract many butterflies and hummingbirds in summer. Breeding warbler populations include olive, red-faced, Grace's, Virginia's, black-throated gray and yellow-rumped warblers and painted redstart. During migration foraging, mixed flocks of warblers will also often include Nashville, Townsend's and hermit warblers. Many high elevation reptiles and amphibians also live in the area, including the diminutive twin-spotted rattlesnake, black-tailed rattlesnake, Slevin's bunch grass lizard and Yarrow's spiny lizard.

Audubon
IMPORTANT
BIRD AREAS

Trails

This recreation area is the trailhead to the Crest Trail complex, where trails range from moderate to difficult and extend for several miles.

Directions From Portal, go west on Forest Road 42 for about 12 miles to Onion Saddle; turn south on Forest Road 42D for 3 miles to the campground. From Willcox, go east on Hwy. 186 for 35 miles toward Chiricahua National Monument entrance; before the entrance, turn southeast on Forest Road 42 for 12 miles to Onion Saddle. Follow the signs to Rustler Park Campground.

Contact U.S.D.A. Forest Service, Coronado National Forest; 520-364-3468; www.fs.fed.us/r3/coronado/forest/recreation/camping/sites/rustler_park.shtml

Features restrooms, trails, motorhome access, parking, picnic area, campgrounds, lookout, trash cans

Sierra Vista Environmental Operations Park

100

Description

These constructed wetlands are part of Sierra Vista's water reclamation facility and attract a large number of birds. Nearly 50 acres of wetlands can be seen from the wildlife-viewing platform.

Wildlife to Watch

Birds commonly seen in the wetlands include various species of waterbirds, white-faced ibis, red-winged and yellow-headed blackbirds, Virginia rail, sora, song sparrow, common yellowthroat and many species of swallows. Mammals commonly seen include bobcat, black-tailed jackrabbit, desert cottontail, mule deer and javelina.

Trails

Access to viewing platform is along main entrance road; there are no other established trails

Site Notes The facility is open to the public daily from 7 a.m.–3 p.m.

Directions Located between mile marker 324 and 325 on north side of SR 90 East, near Sierra Vista.

Contact city of Sierra Vista

Features restrooms, trash cans, trails, overlooks, interpretive signs, brochure/species list, bus/motorhome access, parking, viewing platform

Sweetwater Wetlands
101

Description

Sweetwater Wetlands is an excellent example of a constructed wetland designed to be highly accessible to visitors. It is one of the prime places in urban Tucson to see native wildlife. The 18-acre wetlands provide guided tours and educational programs for school groups and other visitors.

Wildlife to Watch

Over 200 species of birds have been observed at the wetlands, including verdin, vermilion flycatcher, common yellowthroat, Abert's towhee, song sparrow, marsh wren, Harris's hawk and many species of swallows, rails, grebes, herons, shorebirds and waterbirds. The isolated "green spot" also attracts many migratory songbirds. Mammals include desert cottontail, coyote, Arizona cottonrat, round-tailed ground squirrel and rock squirrel. Reptiles include western diamond-backed rattlesnake, desert spiny and zebra-tailed lizards.

Trails

Trails are wide and flat, with one area of gentle inclines. There are universally accessible trails around ponds and through other vegetated areas.

Site Notes Tucson Audubon Society periodically conducts free birding trips for the public to the wetlands.

Directions From eastbound I-10, exit onto the frontage road at the Prince Road exit in Tucson. Immediately move to the right lane and turn right on Sweetwater Drive. Look for Sweetwater Wetlands parking on the left after about 1/10 mile.

Contact Tucson Water; 520-791-5080

Features restrooms, trash cans, trails, overlooks, interpretive signs, brochure/species list, bus/motorhome access, parking, observation deck

SKY ISLANDS ■ Other Sites

Other sites

Dazzling Hummingbirds

With their diminutive size, rapid flight, and typically long slender bills, hummingbirds are some of the most distinctive and admired species in the bird world. Arizona is well known for its spectacular hummingbirds, such as the broad-tailed (at left). Many birders and photographers travel from all over the country (and world) to various locations in the state to witness the sometimes overwhelming concentration of these unique birds. There have been 18 species of hummingbirds observed in Arizona, with 14 of these occurring regularly, particularly in mountain canyons in the southeastern corner of the state. Only Texas can claim this same high number of hummingbird species. They range in size from the tiny calliope hummingbird (the smallest bird in the United States) to the much larger magnificent and blue-throated hummingbirds. Many species are primarily Mexican in origin and extend their range barely into the United States in southeastern Arizona.

Hummingbirds breed in almost every habitat and region of the state. The unique desert-nesting Costa's hummingbird has evolved to breed primarily during the late winter and spring to avoid much of the relentless summer heat. Other species nesting in cool mountain canyons and on forested mountain slopes nest throughout the summer and occasionally into the early fall. Hummingbirds occur throughout the state during their migration, with some traveling from as far north as Alaska and western Canada and south through Mexico. During this period, unbelievable numbers often concentrate at feeding stations with multiple sugar-water feeders. During late summer and early fall, 10–12 species can regularly be observed in a single day at a few favorite locations among the hundreds that continue to zip in and out. Within the United States, only in southeastern Arizona can one routinely observe this many species of hummingbirds at a single location.

Arizona's Coues White-tailed Deer

The white-tailed deer that occurs in Arizona, the Coues white-tail, is one of the smallest of the white-tailed deer, typically weighing 80–100 pounds as adults. Their light gray coats and secretive habits give them the alternate moniker, "The Grey Ghost."

Although referred to as a white-tailed deer, the white tail is not evident unless the animal is alarmed. When startled, the deer raises its otherwise grey tail to expose the white underside, often referred to as "flagging."

Coues white-tailed deer live throughout central to southeastern Arizona. These deer are browsers that primarily occupy oak-savannah habitats, although they live in chaparral and ponderosa pine habitats in some localities. Habitat with steep topographic relief is preferred by the Coues white-tail deer over the more level terrain preferred by Arizona's more abundant mule deer. Though white-tailed deer will at times consume a substantial amount of grass (primarily when fresh and green), they generally consume a varied diet of browse plants. These plants include mesquite, jojoba, fairy duster, ocotillo, oak (acorns), manzanita (berries) and other palatable shrubs.

The grey color and small size make the Coues white-tail deer difficult for the wildlife watcher to view. So take your time. Fort Huachuca is a good site to see Coues white-tailed deer.

White-tailed deer, especially bucks, are probably the easiest to observe during the rut or breeding season. In Arizona, this is typically during late December and January. Gestation is about six months, and young are generally born in July and August. Twins are common, but mortality is generally high during the first few months. Predators of Coues white-tailed deer include mountain lions, coyotes and bobcats, and fawns are more susceptible than are adults to predation.

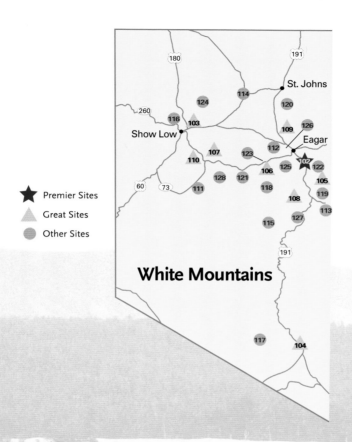

White Mountains

Premier Sites
Great Sites
Other Sites

White Mountains

The band of mountains and valleys running roughly northwest to southeast through the middle of Arizona ends in the White Mountains region of east-central Arizona. Thus, geologists consider the White Mountains part of the transition zone between the Colorado Plateau geological region (to the north) and the Basin and Range geological region (to the south). The high-elevation White Mountains are forested with aspen, pine, spruce and fir. These are interspersed with high-elevation grasslands and broad, open meadows. Just to the west, the Mogollon Rim defines the southern edge of the Colorado Plateau.

PHOTO BY GEORGE ANDREJKO

Beautiful high-elevation scenery; elk and antelope in open meadows

Rufous Hummingbird

PHOTO BY BRUCE D. TAUBERT

Description

This must-see wildlife area offers excellent wildlife viewing and photography, as well as a stunning vista of Arizona's third-highest mountain, Escudilla Mountain, and dramatic examples of petroglyphs. In mid-September through early October, the north slope of Escudilla, five miles away, is covered in yellow and gold aspens. As the leaves turn, the elk begin their breeding season and their wailing bugle can be heard during early morning and dusk. The lucky visitor may even hear the howl of one of the reintroduced Mexican gray wolves. Four hiking trails through a variety of habitats, as well as a visitor center and a day-use picnic area, offer much to the visitor. Habitats include several reservoirs, a stream, wetlands, irrigated meadows and pastures, upland grasslands and pinyon-juniper woodlands. A 50-room, prehistoric ruin that was occupied by ancestral Pueblo people beginning about 1225 A.D. can be seen on the Rudd Creek Trail. The rock outcroppings in the area provide several examples of ancestral Puebloan petroglyphs.

WHITE MOUNTAINS ■ Sipe White Mountain Wildlife Area

Premier
★ SITE ★

Wildlife to Watch

The grasslands feature abundant elk and pronghorn, along with mule deer and coyote. Small mammals include porcupine, badger, Abert's squirrel, golden-mantled and thirteen-lined ground squirrels, long-tailed weasel, cliff chipmunk and striped skunk. Bat species include the cave myotis, long-eared myotis, long-legged myotis, occult little brown, Allen's lappet-browed, silver-haired and hoary bats. Rufous, broad-tailed and calliope hummingbirds are common in July and August. The visitor center has hummingbird feeders, and numerous hummingbirds can be seen at close range. The best birding location at Sipe is along Rudd Creek and in the orchard and tall trees around the visitor center. Songbirds include mountain and western bluebirds, spotted towhee, northern flicker, western wood-pewee, Say's phoebe, white-breasted nuthatch, American robin, Virginia's warbler, black-headed grosbeak and Bullock's oriole. Waterbirds include northern pintail, cinnamon and green-winged teals, redhead, bufflehead, common merganser, mallard, American wigeon, gadwall, Canada goose, white-faced ibis, great blue heron, and pied-billed and eared grebes. Merriam's turkey, Montezuma quail and band-tailed pigeon can also be found in the area. Reptiles and amphibians include prairie rattlesnake, Arizona black rattlesnake, terrestrial gartersnake, gopher snake, greater short-horned lizard, eastern collared lizard, many-lined skink, Arizona treefrog, western chorus frog and tiger salamander.

Trails

There are four hiking trails of easy to moderate difficulty, each with interpretive signs. Trailheads for three of the four trails are adjacent to the parking areas.

Trinity Trail 350 yards, universally accessible, leads to a wildlife-viewing point adjacent to Trinity Reservoir.

High Point Loop Trail 1 mile, moderate difficulty, viewing points with benches, spotting scope for observing large mammals in the meadows below.

Rudd Creek Loop Trail 3 miles, mostly flat terrain, several wildlife viewing points and benches.

Homestead Trail 1½-mile spur trail (3 miles total) over flat terrain to the Nelson cabin homestead.

Site Notes Hunting occurs at this site from late August to mid-December.

Size 1,362 acres

Directions From Eagar, take U.S. Hwy. 180/191 southeast toward Alpine. Look for turnoff signs immediately at the top of the first mesa at milepost 404.7. Follow the graded dirt road 5 miles to the wildlife area.

Nearest Town Eagar

Ownership Arizona Game and Fish Department

Contact 928-367-4281
www.azgfd.gov/outdoor_recreation/wildlife_area_sipe.shtml

Features restrooms, trash cans, trails, lookouts, interpretive signs, brochures, visitor center, drinking water, bus/motorhome access, parking, spotting scope, picnic area

Rocky Mountain Elk

PHOTO BY JOE AND MARISA CERRETA

Arizona Treefrog

PHOTO BY RANDY BABB

Premier
★ SITE ★

Allen Severson Memorial Wildlife Area/Pintail Lake

Created waterfowl habitat close to rural communities

Allen Severson Memorial Wildlife Area/Pintail Lake

PHOTO BY GEORGE ANDREJKO

Description

The city of Show Low, in cooperation with the U.S.D.A. Forest Service and Arizona Game and Fish Department, became the first Arizona community and one of the first in the nation to create artificial wetlands for the disposal of wastewater effluent. The scarcity of marshland ecosystems in the arid southwest made projects like Pintail Lake, a 370-acre marsh, vital to Arizona bird populations.

Pintail Lake's objectives were to increase waterfowl production by creating lakes with nesting islands and to provide wastewater disposal for the city of Show Low. This site offers interpretive information at the observation platform and blind, as well as a self-guided trail with several interpretive signs.

Wildlife to Watch

Many birds are attracted to the marsh surrounded by pinyon-juniper habitat. Look for waterfowl such as cinnamon teal, ruddy duck, ring-necked duck, gadwall, bufflehead, American wigeon and northern pintail. Other wetland birds include black-crowned night-heron, white-faced ibis, American avocet, black-necked stilt, long-billed dowitcher, sora, Virginia rail, yellow-headed and red-winged blackbirds and great blue heron. Keep an eye on the snags and in the air for various birds of prey, which could include bald eagle (in winter), osprey, red-tailed hawk, northern harrier and prairie falcon.

Pinyon-juniper grasslands surround the wetland, offering observations of Townsend's solitaire, gray vireo, juniper titmouse and mountain chickadee. In addition to birds, look for elk, mule deer and pronghorn, as well as eastern collared and southwestern fence lizards, terrestrial gartersnake and tarantula.

Trails

There is a ¼-mile level, paved trail from the parking area to the enclosed viewing blind; a short 30-yard concrete trail leads from paved trail near the enclosed blind to an open observation deck; both trails are universally accessible.

Site Notes Observation platform.

Size 370 acres

Directions From Show Low, drive north on State Hwy. 77 for approximately 3 miles. Turn east at Allen Severson Memorial Wildlife Memorial Area (Pintail Lake) sign and continue on dirt road approximately ½ mile to cindered parking area.

Nearest Town Show Low

Ownership U.S.D.A. Forest Service, Apache-Sitgreaves National Forests

Contact 928-368-5111
www.fs.fed.us/r3/asnf

Features trash cans, trails, covered observation deck, interpretive signs, brochure/bird species list, bus/motorhome access, photo blinds, parking

Northern Pintail

PHOTO BY BRUCE D. TAUBERT

WHITE MOUNTAINS ■ Allen Severson Memorial Wildlife Area/Pintail Lake

Great
▲ SITE ▲

Coronado Trail

PHOTO BY GEORGE ANDREJKO

Description

The Mogollon Rim stretches across east-central Arizona, and the Coronado Trail (Highway 191) travels up to and across the Mogollon Rim. The highway is officially designated a National, State and Forest Service Scenic Byway. The highway provides spectacular views of the Mogollon Rim, the Gila Wilderness and the San Carlos Apache Reservation. It ranges in elevation from 3,500 to over 9,000 feet, and is 123 miles long.

Visitors drive through high desert, pinyon-juniper woodlands, open grassland meadows, ponderosa pine and mixed conifer forests to high alpine meadows. The variety of habitats and the remoteness of the landscape make for excellent wildlife viewing. There are interpretive displays on wildlife, the effects of fire and topography along the roadway. The road passes by North America's largest copper mine in Morenci, Arizona. The Red Mountain Interpretive Fire Display presents information on the use of wild and prescribed fires in the management of National Forest Lands. There are interpretive panels about Mexican gray wolf recovery at the Blue Vista Lookout.

Wildlife to Watch

Look for pronghorn in the open grassland around Springerville. Elk, Merriam's turkey, and Abert's and red squirrels can be seen in the forested areas around Alpine and Hannagan Meadow, which is also home to the reintroduced Mexican gray wolf. Active beaver dams can be found in the creeks along the highway. With the wide range of elevations and subsequent habitats along this route, over 200 breeding species of birds can be encountered, including plumbeous vireo, pygmy nuthatch, Williamson's sapsucker and spotted towhee. White-tailed deer are found in the lower, southern elevations. There is a very good possibility of seeing bighorn sheep in the Morenci Mine area.

Between Springerville and Alpine is Nelson Reservoir, an excellent site for viewing waterfowl and bald eagles during winter months and osprey during summer months.

Trails

There are no trails associated with auto loop; however, there are numerous hiking trails in area.

Site Notes	The Coronado Trail has numerous sharp curves and is very steep; drivers should take extra caution when navigating its contours.
Size	123-mile drive
Directions	Start on the Coronado Trail on U.S. Hwy. 191 at either Clifton on the south or Eagar on the north.
Nearest Town	Clifton or Eagar
Ownership	Department of Transportation
Contact	520-670-4552
Features	restrooms, trash cans, trails, lookouts, interpretive signs, brochure/bird species list, bus/motorhome access, boat ramps, parking, picnic areas

Williamson's Sapsucker   PHOTO BY BRIAN E. SMALL

Great
▲ SITE ▲

105

Escudilla Mountain-Terry Flat Loop

Magnificent fall colors atop one of Arizona's highest peaks

Escudilla Mountain-Terry Flat Loop

PHOTO BY GEORGE ANDREJKO

Description

This 15-mile driving route along the eastern edge of the White Mountains loops around the high meadows of Escudilla Mountain, the third highest peak in Arizona at 10,912 feet elevation. There are old-growth stands of Engleman spruce, aspen, and Douglas and white fir in the nearby Escudilla Wilderness Area. Extensive groves of aspen provide magnificent fall colors mid-September through early October. Sego lily, Indian paintbrush, cinquefoil and wild onions are among the abundant wildflowers in July and August. The Escudilla Wilderness Area encompasses a hiking trail on top of Escudilla Mountain.

Wildlife to Watch

Wildlife can be viewed along the entire length of the drive or from the hiking trail. Elk, mule deer, Merriam's turkey, blue grouse, black bear, long-tailed weasel, and Abert's and red squirrels are commonly seen, along with many songbirds. Look for broad-tailed and rufous hummingbirds, Williamson's and red-naped sapsuckers, Cordilleran flycatcher and plumbeous vireo. Mountain bluebird, western tanager, hermit thrush, Clark's nutcracker, golden-crowned kinglet, dark-eyed junco and northern goshawk are among the many birds seen here. Terry Flat is a reliable place to find an American three-toed woodpecker. Take the right fork of the loop and listen for the three-toed woodpecker's drumming, especially near the Paddy Creek area.

WHITE MOUNTAINS ■ Escudilla Mountain-Terry Flat Loop

Great
▲ SITE ▲

Trails

The 6-mile Terry Flat loop can be driven or walked. Escudilla National Recreation Trail #308 is three miles in length with a moderate difficulty rating, traversing the wilderness area from the loop road to the fire tower on the mountain summit. Once topping out from the highway, take the left fork of the loop road about ⅓ mile to the trailhead parking area.

Size	15-mile loop drive
Directions	From Alpine, go north on U.S. Hwy. 191 almost 6 miles and then turn east at Milepost 421 onto Forest Road 56 (Terry Flat-Hulsey Lake road). Continue for 4⁷⁄₁₀ miles to the road fork that begins the 6-mile loop of Terry Flat atop Escudilla Mountain.
Nearest Town	Alpine
Ownership	U.S.D.A. Forest Service, Apache Sitgreaves National Forests
Contact	928-339-4384 www.fs.fed.us/r3/asnf
Features	trails, parking

American Three-toed Woodpecker   PHOTO BY BRIAN E. SMALL

WHITE MOUNTAINS ■ Escudilla Mountain-Terry Flat Loop

Great
▲ SITE ▲

106

Greer

Great birding and hiking opportunities in a scenic mountain community

Greer

PHOTO BY GEORGE ANDREJKO

Description

At approximately 8,600 feet elevation, this small community rarely exceeds temperatures of 75° F in the hottest months. The beautiful summer scenery makes hiking and wildlife viewing a pleasant experience. The Little Colorado River flows through Greer, and there are three nearby reservoirs known for trout fishing. Squirrel Spring Recreation Area is 2½ miles from the junction with State Hwy. 260. The riparian areas at Squirrel Spring Recreation Area and the Little Colorado River are good examples of willow habitat, while the Butler Canyon Trail offers ponderosa pine forest habitat.

Wildlife to Watch

Mammals in the area include black bear, elk, mule and white-tailed deer, pronghorn, coyote, Abert's and red squirrel, beaver and muskrat. Terrestrial gartersnakes are common in the dense vegetation along the river. This area provides some of the best summer birding opportunities in the White Mountains, with several uncommon and locally nesting birds such as dusky and willow flycatchers, Clark's nutcracker, gray catbird, green-tailed towhee, Lincoln's sparrow and golden-crowned kinglet. Summer warblers can include the yellow-rumped, Grace's, red-faced, MacGillivray's and Virginia's. Osprey, double-crested cormorant and great blue heron nest along River Reservoir. A wide range of waterfowl can also be seen including Canada goose, common merganser, mallard and cinnamon teal. Look for the American dipper and spotted sandpiper foraging in the rocky areas in the Little Colorado River.

Trails

Hiking trails traverse various habitat types, including river and lake riparian, ponderosa pine, spruce-fir and aspen. The East Fork Trail, accessed from the first parking lot south of the cattle guard, has a difficult rating, is several miles in length and climbs from 8,200 to 9,300 feet before leveling out. The Butler Canyon Trail is self-guided. The Forest Service conducts interpretive lectures and walks during the summer. Activity schedules are posted at Hoyer campground and at the Springerville Ranger Station. Access the website below for additional information.

Site Notes	There is private property interspersed with the public land in the Greer area; please respect it and do not trespass.
Size	2,120 acres
Directions	Travel west 10½ miles from Eagar on State Hwy. 260 to State Hwy. 373. Follow Hwy. 373 south a few miles to the Greer area.
Nearest Town	Greer
Ownership	U.S.D.A. Forest Service, Apache-Sitgreaves National Forests
Contact	928-333-4372 www.fs.fed.us/r3/asnf
Features	restrooms, trash cans, trails, interpretive signs, bus/motorhome access, boat ramps, parking, campgrounds, picnic areas

Green-tailed Towhee PHOTO BY BRUCE D. TAUBERT

WHITE MOUNTAINS ■ Greer

Great
▲ SITE ▲

A man-made marsh within pinyon-juniper woodland

Jacques Marsh

PHOTO BY BRUCE SITKO

Description

In 1978, the Town of Pinetop/Lakeside initiated construction of a marsh complex to treat wastewater effluent. Cooperators included the U.S.D.A. Forest Service, Pinetop/Lakeside Sanitary District, and Arizona Game and Fish Department, who agreed to maintain the area for waterfowl habitat. This site offers a 130-acre marshland surrounded by pinyon-juniper woodland and seven ponds with 18 islands for bird nesting habitat. The topography is gentle rolling land with a northerly slope. The vegetative communities are predominately pinyon-juniper woodland and deciduous woodland.

Wildlife to Watch

The marsh area attracts a variety of wildlife, including wetland birds, mule deer, elk, bald eagle (during winter months) and other birds of prey, and songbirds. Permanent resident birds include Bewick's wren and belted kingfisher. Bank swallow and purple martin can be seen during migration periods. In the summer, sora and yellow-headed blackbird are common in cattails. Open areas in the grassland provide habitat for loggerhead shrike, western kingbird, western bluebird, northern mockingbird, and vesper, lark and savannah sparrows. Woodlands surrounding the ponds contain species such as white-breasted nuthatch, juniper titmouse and black-throated warbler. Waterfowl that have been observed include mallard, northern pintail, redhead, bufflehead, canvasback and green-winged and cinnamon teals. Other wildlife includes

WHITE MOUNTAINS ■ *Jacques Marsh*

Great
▲ SITE ▲

Gunnison's prairie dog, southwestern fence lizard, gopher snake, terrestrial gartersnake, eastern collared lizard, greater short-horned lizard and tarantula.

Trails

There are no formal trails.

Size	130 acres
Directions	From the traffic light at the junction of State Hwy. 260 and Penrod Road in Lakeside, proceed north 1½ miles on Penrod Road to Juniper Drive. Take this dirt side street through a residential area and over a cattle guard. Follow the road curving to the right and over a second cattle guard to a parking lot and information kiosk ⁷⁄₁₀ mile from Penrod Road.
Nearest Town	Pinetop/Lakeside
Ownership	U.S.D.A. Forest Service, Apache-Sitgreaves National Forests
Contact	928-368-5111 www.fs.fed.us/r3/asnf
Features	trash cans, brochure/bird species list, parking

Yellow-headed Blackbird

PHOTO BY BRUCE D. TAUBERT

WHITE MOUNTAINS ▪ *Jacques Marsh*

Great
▲ SITE ▲

Water Canyon-Big Lake Loop Drive

PHOTO BY BRUCE SITKO

Description

This 45-mile scenic driving loop passes through high-elevation grassland, ponderosa pine and mixed-conifer forests, and wetland and river riparian habitats. There are excellent views of subalpine grasslands along the entire route; lake and marsh vistas at Salt House Marsh, Big Lake, Crescent Lake and Mexican Hay Lake; and a scenic overlook of Great Basin grasslands to the north at Point of the Mountain rest stop. This is an easy drive with many pull-outs and facilities along the way.

Wildlife to Watch

Large and small mammals are easily seen from vehicles, especially at sunrise or sunset. These can include elk, mule deer, pronghorn, coyote, long-tailed weasel and golden-mantled ground squirrel. Abert's and red squirrels are common. Birds of prey include bald eagle, turkey vulture, osprey, American kestrel, northern goshawk, and red-tailed, Cooper's and sharp-shinned hawks. Summer residents include violet-green swallow, Cordilleran flycatcher and plumbeous vireo. In marsh areas, look for great blue heron, belted kingfisher, red-winged and yellow-headed blackbirds, and a variety of waterfowl. Bird species in grassland habitats include western and mountain bluebirds, horned lark, eastern and western meadowlarks, vesper and savannah sparrows, northern harrier and an occasional golden eagle. Mixed-conifer and spruce-fir forest birds include red crossbill, pine siskin, red-breasted nuthatch, American three-toed woodpecker, western tanager, golden- and ruby-crowned kinglets,

Great
▲ SITE ▲

yellow-rumped warbler, Clark's nutcracker and the very local gray jay. Look in aspen stands for Williamson's and red-naped sapsuckers and blue grouse. Pine grosbeak are occasionally seen around the Big Lake area.

Trails

There are no trails associated with auto loop; however, there are numerous hiking trails in the area. Check Forest Service website below.

Site Notes	A Forest Service visitor center at the Big Lake Recreation Area is open during summer months, located approximately 1 mile south of Forest Road 113 on FR 113A. It offers complete, accessible facilities and free interpretive programs. Inquire at the Springerville Ranger District for date, time and topic.
Size	45-mile driving loop
Directions	At junction of Hwys. 60 and 180/191 in Springerville, proceed south on Main Street through Eagar to the sawmill, turning left on Water Canyon Road (Hwy. 285). Continue south for 21 miles to the junction of FR 285 and 249. Turn right on FR 249 and drive $\frac{7}{10}$ mile to the junction with FR 113. Take FR 113 another 3 miles, past the Big Lake turnoff (FR 115) and Crescent Lake, to the junction with State Hwy. 261. Follow State Hwy. 261 18$\frac{1}{2}$ miles to the intersection with State Hwy. 260, 3 miles west of Eagar.
Nearest Town	Springerville/Eagar
Ownership	U.S.D.A. Forest Service, Apache-Sitgreaves National Forests
Contact	928-333-4372 www.fs.fed.us/r3/asnf
Features	restrooms, trash cans, lookouts, visitor center, bus/motorhome access, parking, campgrounds, picnic areas

American Pronghorn

PHOTO BY BRUCE D. TAUBERT

WHITE MOUNTAINS ■ *Water Canyon-Big Lake Loop Drive*

Great
▲ SITE ▲

109

Wenima Wildlife Area

Petroglyphs and birds in a riparian willow corridor

Wenima Wildlife Area

PHOTO BY GEORGE ANDREJKO

Description

Wenima Wildlife Area features a corridor of willow riparian habitat along the Little Colorado River, one of the few such sites in the state that is open to the public. In addition, wetland and floodplains, upland pinyon-juniper, grassland and canyon cliff habitats attract a wide range of species and some unusual bird species, such as the gray catbird, a very local nesting species in Arizona.

Small areas of petroglyphs from prehistoric cultures that occupied the area from 1275 to 1400 A.D. can be found along the trails.

Wildlife to Watch

The riparian corridor stretches for two miles along the Little Colorado River. Mammals include mule deer, eastern cottontail, black-tailed jackrabbit, coyote and rock squirrel. There are opportunities to see American kestrel, yellow-breasted chat, black phoebe, mountain and western bluebirds, mallard, American wigeon, great blue heron, and a variety of migrating warblers and other songbirds. The walnut trees and willow thickets are particularly attractive to migrants. It is also possible to see yellow-billed cuckoo, Lewis's woodpecker, belted kingfisher, blue grosbeak and black-crowned night-heron. Black phoebe and spotted sandpiper can often be found along the drainage. Reptiles and amphibians include prairie rattlesnake, terrestrial gartersnake, eastern collared lizard, greater short-horned lizard and Arizona toad.

Audubon
IMPORTANT
BIRD AREAS

Great
▲ SITE ▲

Trails

Two easy-walking dirt trails parallel the Little Colorado River. Powerhouse Trail runs south along the east bank of the river for ¾ mile. Beavertail Trail runs north along the west bank of the river for 1½ miles. Both trails are self-guided, with interpretive signage.

Site Notes Year round access with best birding and photography in spring, summer and fall.

Size 357 acres

Directions At the junction of U.S. Hwys. 60 and 180/191, go ¼ mile north on Hwy. 180/191 and turn right on a graded dirt road. After 1½ miles, the road drops a short distance into the Little Colorado River canyon corridor.

Nearest Town Springerville

Ownership Arizona Game and Fish Department

Contact 928-367-4281
www.azgfd.gov/outdoor_recreation/wildlife_area_wenima.shtml

Features restroom, trash cans, trails, interpretive signs, parking, picnic area

Lewis's Woodpecker PHOTO BY TOM VEZO

Great
▲ SITE ▲

110

Woodland Lake Park and Big Springs Environmental Area

Easy wildlife viewing and photography in a mountain town

Woodland Lake Park and Big Springs Environmental Area

PHOTO BY BRUCE SITKO

Description

Woodland Lake Park, nestled in the middle of the Town of Pinetop-Lakeside, provides exceptional wildlife viewing experiences. The site has open water, marshland, ponderosa pine, Gambel oak and juniper forests. There are numerous trails, including a paved trail, picnic areas with ramadas, a man-made lake, interpretive signage and benches. Wildlife at this site are accustomed to human presence and are easy to view and photograph from trails. Big Springs Environmental Area is connected to the park with a well-designed trail system. The area was developed for environmental education purposes for local schools and includes interpretive trail signage.

Wildlife to Watch

Walking the Lake Loop Trail in the summer provides opportunity to see osprey, turkey vulture, doubled-crested cormorant, pied-billed grebe, great blue heron, belted kingfisher and Wilson's snipe. Lewis's and acorn woodpeckers, dark-eyed junco and ruby-crowned kinglet are regulars. In spring and summer months, look for common yellowthroat, red-winged and yellow-headed blackbirds, chipping sparrow, broad-tailed and rufous hummingbirds, lesser goldfinch, yellow-rumped warbler, house wren, purple martin, western tanager, western and mountain bluebirds, mountain chickadee, white-breasted and pygmy nuthatches, brown creeper, and violet-green, barn, tree and northern rough-winged swallows. In the winter months, look for bald eagle, bufflehead, American wigeon, canvasback, ring-necked duck, cedar waxwing and white-

Great
▲ SITE ▲

crowned sparrow. Spring is a good time to see cinnamon teal and ruddy ducks in their colorful breeding plumage. Osprey utilize the lake in the summer, perching on the numerous snags surrounding the lake and diving for fish.

Trails

A variety of trails is found within the Woodland Lake Park system. The Lake Loop Trail is approximately one mile in length. The Hitching Post Loop is two miles long and leads to the Big Springs area. Other trails on this site are dirt packed and provide good hiking and mountain biking.

Size 580 acres

Directions From the intersection of Hwy. 260 and Woodland Lake Road in east Pinetop, proceed west ¼ mile on Woodland Lake Road to the park entrance on the right. Follow the paved road through the park entrance to the parking area adjacent to the lake.

Nearest Town Pinetop/Lakeside

Ownership U.S.D.A. Forest Service/managed by town of Pinetop/Lakeside

Contact 928-368-5111
www.ci.pinetop-lakeside.az.us/woodland.shtml

Features restrooms, trash cans, trails, interpretive signs, brochure/bird species list, drinking water, bus/motorhome access, boat ramps, parking, fishing pier and trail around lake (both universally accessible), picnic areas with ramadas

Osprey PHOTO BY BRIAN E. SMALL

Great
▲ SITE ▲

Alchesay National Fish Hatchery 111

Description

Alchesay National Fish Hatchery is located in the picturesque canyon of the North Fork of the White River on the Fort Apache Indian Reservation at an elevation of 5,400 feet. Self-guided tours of the hatchery are offered.

Wildlife to Watch

Bald eagle, osprey, common merganser, ring-necked duck and bufflehead can reliably be seen here during fall and winter. Common summer birds include great blue heron, broad-tailed hummingbird, rufous hummingbird, acorn woodpecker and Merriam's turkey.

Trails

There are no formal trails.

Site Notes When traveling through Native American lands, observe tribal regulations.

Directions Travel east from Pinetop/Lakeside on State Hwy. 260 for 2 miles to the Hon-Dah junction. Turn south on State Hwy. 73, go 15 miles to the Alchesay NFH Road. Turn east and follow the signs 4 miles to the hatchery.

Contact U.S. Fish and Wildlife Service; 928-338-4901; www.fws.gov/fisheries/nfhs/awc.htm

Features restrooms, trash cans, interpretive signs, brochure/bird species list, drinking water, bus/motorhome access, picnic area, parking

Be sure to visit Williams Creek National Fish Hatchery located adjacent to this site.

Becker Lake Wildlife Area 112

Description

Becker Lake was created in 1880 by building a dam across an old oxbow of the Little Colorado River. Today, this shallow reservoir rimmed by wetlands and surrounded by high-elevation grasslands offers excellent birding and wildlife viewing.

Wildlife to Watch

Mammals include mule deer, occasional pronghorn, Gunnison's prairie dog and rock squirrels. Birds of prey include bald eagle (during winter months), osprey, American kestrel, prairie falcon, northern harrier, red-tailed hawk and turkey vulture. Among the waterfowl are nesting Canada goose, mallard, cinnamon teal and ruddy duck. Migration and winter bring rarer species such as tundra swan and Barrow's goldeneye. During August and September, the grassland east of the lake attracts migrating rufous, broad-tailed and calliope hummingbirds.

Trails

Two dirt hiking trails offer easy access for wildlife viewing. The Lakeview Trail is a 1-mile loop to an observation platform at the south end of the lake. The River Walk Trail parallels the Little Colorado River.

Directions Becker Lake is 2 miles west of the traffic light in Springerville at the junction of Hwys. 60 and 260; turn south and follow signs.

Contact Arizona Game and Fish Department; 928-367-4281
www.azgfd.gov/outdoor_recreation/wildlife_area_becker.shtml

Features restrooms, trash cans, trails, viewing platform, interpretive signs, bus/motorhome access, boat ramps, parking

Blue River Drive   113

Description

This 30-mile driving route (one way), or 48-mile loop for high clearance vehicles, passes through exceptional river riparian habitat along one of the last undammed and least-populated rivers in the Southwest. Because of its location and elevation changes, the Blue River area is one of the most interesting birding areas in east-central Arizona.

Wildlife to Watch

Look for bighorn sheep on the slopes of the Red Hill area along Forest Road 567, about 3½ miles northwest of the Blue River. In the Blue Range Primitive Area, the Mexican gray wolf has been reintroduced. Large mammals include elk, mule and white-tailed deer, black bear and javelina. Birders can look for Montezuma quail, common nighthawk, white-throated swift, peregrine falcon, Cooper's and sharp-shinned hawks and Townsend's solitaire.

Audubon
IMPORTANT
BIRD AREAS

Trails

There are more than 25 hiking trails with trailheads that originate on the Blue River corridor. Detailed information on these trails can be obtained from the Apache-Sitgreaves National Forests' web site below.

Directions From the intersection with U.S. Hwy. 191 in Alpine, travel 3½ miles east on U.S. Hwy. 180 to junction of Forest Road 281, located at western edge of Luna Lake. Take FR 281 south; after approximately 5 miles, it will meet and parallel the Blue River for 25 more miles before it dead-ends at private property. Visitors may retrace their route back to Hwy. 180.

Contact U.S.D.A. Forest Service, Apache-Sitgreaves National Forests; www.fs.fed.us/r3/asnf

Features restrooms, trails, lookouts, parking, campgrounds

Concho Lake   114

Description

Concho Lake, at 6,300 feet elevation, is a popular 208-acre fishing and birding site, harboring abundant waterfowl, resident and migratory birds. Birding is the primary wildlife viewing activity from the lake shoreline or in surrounding vegetation.

WHITE MOUNTAINS ■ *Other Sites*

Other sites

221

Wildlife to Watch

A wide range of migratory waterfowl includes Clark's and western grebes, Canada goose, and ducks including ring-necked duck, common goldeneye, gadwall, bufflehead, canvasback, northern shoveler and others. Bald eagles can be seen in fall and winter, as well as horned lark, western meadowlark and northern mockingbird. Other common birds include spotted sandpiper, killdeer and a variety of sparrows. This is a reliable place to see American pipit during migration.

Directions The lake is located in Concho on the south side of Hwy. 61. Concho is 27 miles northeast of Show Low and 15 miles west of St. Johns.

Contact Arizona Game and Fish Department; 928-367-4281

Features restrooms, trash cans, bus/motorhome access, boat ramps, parking

Fish Creek Trail   115

Description

The 5½-mile Fish Creek Trail drops into a narrow forested canyon from a high bench that overlooks both the Black River and Fish Creek drainages. Once on the floor of the canyon, the trail wanders downstream along Fish Creek past pools, riffles and stepping-stone stream crossings to the point where this tributary joins the Black River.

Wildlife to Watch

Fish Creek harbors a population of Arizona's state fish, the Apache trout. You may see black bear, elk, mule deer, porcupine, Abert's squirrel, golden-mantled ground squirrel, Merriam's turkey, northern goshawk, peregrine falcon, Mexican spotted owl, and an amazing variety of resident and migratory songbirds. Reptiles and amphibians of the area include Arizona treefrog, western chorus frog, northern leopard frog, greater short-horned lizard, plateau striped whiptail, Madrean alligator lizard, ring-necked snake, narrow-headed gartersnake, Sonoran mountain kingsnake and Arizona black rattlesnake.

Directions From Buffalo Crossing, follow FR 24 to FR 83. Turn west and follow FR83 about 3 miles to FR 83A, which turns right about 1⅖ miles to a lesser dirt road which then forks left. Follow this road about ½ miles past an old corral to the trailhead of the Fish Creek Access Trail #320. From here it's ⅗ miles to Fish Creek.

Contact U.S.D.A. Forest Service, Apache-Sitgreaves National Forests; 928-339-4384; www.fs.fed.us/r3/asnf/recreation/alpine_trails/trl_alp_fishcreek.shtml

Features trail, interpretive signs, parking

Fool Hollow Lake Recreation Area   116

Description

The 800-acre Fool Hollow Lake Recreation Area offers year-round wildlife viewing opportunities, as well as camping, fishing, picnicking and boating. A dam on Show Low Creek forms 180-acre Fool Hollow Lake, creating a natural feeding ground for a variety of wildlife.

Wildlife to Watch

Fool Hollow Lake is a very good birding site. Visitors should walk campsite loops and look for common mergansers and other diving ducks on the eastern arm of the lake. During winter months, visitors can often see bald eagles perched on snags. On the west side of the lake, fishing piers are good places to set spotting scopes to view both dabbling and diving ducks. Other water birds that can be observed here include double-crested cormorant, great blue heron, black-crowned night-heron, spotted sandpiper and long-billed dowitcher.

The upland area offers rock wren, dark-eyed junco, pygmy and white-breasted nuthatches and several woodpecker species, like red-naped sapsucker and northern flicker.

Directions From downtown Show Low at the traffic light on Deuce of Clubs and Old Linden Road, travel 2½ miles northwest on Old Linden Road to the signed state park entrance. An alternative route is to take the signed turnoff from Hwy. 260 onto Old Linden Road on the west side of Show Low and travel ½ mile to the park entrance.

Contact Arizona State Parks; 928-537-3680; www.azstateparks.com/Parks/parkhtml/foolhollow.html

Features restrooms, trash cans, bus/motorhome access, boat ramps, fishing piers, picnic areas with armadas, universal accessibility, parking, campgrounds

Honeymoon Campground   117

Description

The access road to this small 20-acre campground transitions from pinyon-juniper woodlands to an open grassland valley with perennial streams and passes many old ranch houses. Views extend into the open grasslands and pine forests, as well as a substantial stretch of the Mogollon Rim face.

Wildlife to Watch

One can see pronghorn, mule and white-tailed deer, elk, common black-hawk, golden eagle and peregrine falcon alongside the roadway. Breeding birds in the area include acorn woodpecker, black phoebe, brown-crested flycatcher, Cassin's kingbird and plumbeous and Hutton's vireos. Hike along Eagle Creek for loach minnow, spikedace and Gila chub.

Trails

Honeymoon Campground provides a starting point for hiking up Eagle Creek to Salt House or Chitty Canyons, as well as to the Malay Gap area. The terrain is steep and rocky. Difficulty level is moderate to difficult.

Directions Take Hwy. 191, the Coronado Trail, north through Clifton, then past the Morenci Copper Mine. Fourteen miles past the Morenci Copper Mine, take Forest Road 217 west along Eagle Creek approximately 22 miles until you reach the road's end, which is Honeymoon Campground.

Contact U.S.D.A. Forest Service, Apache-Sitgreaves National Forests; 928-687-1301; www.fs.fed.us/r3/asnf/recreation/campgrounds/devcamp/devcamp_honeymoon.shtml

Features restrooms, trash cans, trails, brochure/bird species list, parking

WHITE MOUNTAINS ■ Other Sites

Other sites

Lee Valley Reservoir

118

Description

This is a scenic, high-elevation lake at the foot of Mount Baldy with outstanding views. Surrounding the reservoir are open meadows and spruce-fir forests. Near the dam, excess water flows through a natural spillway, creating a wetland marsh. Extensive stands of aspen provide magnificent fall colors.

Wildlife to Watch

Mammals include elk, mule deer, coyote, beaver, thirteen-lined ground squirrel, red squirrel, long-tailed weasel and porcupine. Wetland birds include great blue heron, pied-billed grebe, ring-necked duck, bufflehead and common merganser. Birds of prey such as bald eagle, turkey vulture, osprey, red-tailed hawk and American kestrel are common. During July and August, you may also see broad-tailed, rufous and calliope hummingbirds. Steller's jay, golden-crowned and ruby-crowned kinglets, American three-toed and hairy woodpeckers, and mountain chickadees nest in the surrounding forest.

Trails

There are no formal trails; a rustic footpath circles the reservoir, about one mile in length.

Directions From Eagar, go west on State Hwy. 260 for 3 miles to the junction with State Hwy. 261. Take Hwy. 261 south 18½ miles to the intersection with Forest Road 113. Turn right onto FR 113 and proceed 6 miles west to the turnoff to Lee Valley Reservoir. Turn left and proceed ½ mile to the parking area.

Contact U.S.D.A. Forest Service, Apache-Sitgreaves National Forests; 928-333-4372; www.fs.fed.us/r3/asnf

Features restrooms, bus/motorhome access, boat ramps, parking

Luna Lake

119

Description

Nestled in the White Mountains, the 200-acre site near the south slope of Escudilla Mountain has marsh and lake riparian and ponderosa pine forest habitats.

Wildlife to Watch

This is an excellent site for viewing wetland birds and has an established bald eagle nest site. The grasslands surrounding the lake provide excellent winter foraging habitat for large birds of prey such as ferruginous and occasional rough-legged hawks. Waterbirds include cinnamon teal, northern shoveler, mallard, Canada goose, American coot, spotted sandpiper, great blue heron, sora, Virginia rail and Wilson's snipe. Migratory songbirds abound. Mule deer and elk can be seen watering at the lake during sunrise and sunset hours. Beaver and muskrat are best seen in late evening.

WHITE MOUNTAINS ■ Other Sites

Other sites

224

Site Notes The west portion of the lake and adjacent shoreline is closed to public entry from April 1 to August 1 to provide nesting habitat for waterfowl. There is a closure area north of the lake associated with the bald eagle nest from January 1–June 30. With binoculars, the public can still view eagle and waterfowl activity during either closure.

Directions From Alpine, go east on U.S. Hwy. 180 four miles to turnoff to Luna Lake. Turn north onto Forest Road 570 to access the lake shoreline and the Forest Service campground located on the northeast side of the lake.

Contact U.S.D.A. Forest Service, Apache-Sitgreaves National Forests; 928-339-4384; www.fs.fed.us/r3/asnf

Features restrooms, trash cans, bus/motorhome access, boat ramps, parking, campgrounds

Lyman Lake State Park   120

Description

The 1,200-acre park encompasses the shoreline of Lyman Lake, an irrigation reservoir created by damming the Little Colorado River. At 6,000 feet elevation, Lyman Lake State Park is nestled among several mesas and slopes covered with pinyon pine and juniper woodland, and is fed by snowmelt from the slopes of Mount Baldy and Escudilla Mountain, the second and third highest mountains in Arizona.

Wildlife to Watch

Waterfowl congregate on the lake near the dam; a variety of migrating shorebirds can be found in flooded pockets of grassy areas. Look for American wigeon, lesser scaup, common goldeneye, black-necked stilt, greater and lesser yellowlegs and marbled godwit. Gulls and terns also use the lake during migration. From fall through spring, western and Clark's grebes can be found on the lake, and Barrow's goldeneye has been seen here. Common merganser, double-crested cormorant and a variety of ducks are more common. Several species of flycatchers and swallows are seen in picnic and camping areas during migration. Other birds include canyon and rock wrens, canyon towhee, American kestrel, common yellowthroat, Townsend's solitaire, Bullock's oriole, greater roadrunner, mountain bluebird and pinyon jay. Mammals include pronghorn, cliff chipmunk, golden-mantled ground squirrel, Gunnison's prairie dog and rock squirrels. Reptiles and amphibians include terrestrial gartersnake, greater short-horned lizard and Mexican spadefoot.

Trails

Three trails lead to petroglyph features in the park. Best wildlife viewing is from the lake or the shoreline.

Directions Located 11 miles south of St. Johns on U.S. Hwy. 180/191.

Contact Arizona State Parks; 928-337-4441

Features restrooms, trash cans, bus/motorhome access, boat ramps, picnic areas, universal accessibility, parking, campgrounds

Other sites

Mount Baldy Loop Drive

121

Description

This 36-mile scenic driving loop offers excellent views of high-elevation grasslands along the entire route; river riparian habitat at Sheep's Crossing on the West Fork of the Little Colorado River; lake and marsh vistas at Lee Valley Reservoir, Crescent Lake, Basin Lake Marsh and Mexican Hay Lake; and a scenic overlook of Great Basin grasslands to the north at Point of the Mountain rest stop.

Wildlife to Watch

Large mammals are easily seen from vehicles, especially at sunrise or sunset. There are overlooks at Lee Valley Reservoir and Mexican Hay Lake.

Look for elk, mule deer, pronghorn and coyote, as well as Abert's, golden-mantled and red squirrels. Waterbirds seen here include great blue heron, pied-billed and eared grebes, and ducks such as mallard, ring-necked, American wigeon, bufflehead and common merganser. Many birds of prey are seen at the higher elevations. Birders hiking the West Baldy trail may encounter some of the most local nesting species in Arizona including gray jay, pine grosbeak, Swainson's thrush, orange-crowned and MacGillivray's warblers, Lincoln's sparrow and green-tailed towhee. By carefully checking the creek above and below Sheep Crossing, you may find American dipper.

Audubon
IMPORTANT
BIRD AREAS

Trails

Two hiking trails are available along this loop—West Baldy and East Baldy Trails. Each trail is seven miles in length and parallels a portion of the East or West Fork of the Little Colorado River. The trails meet near the top of Mt. Baldy; the summit is located on the Fort Apache Indian Reservation, and access is closed to non-tribal members.

Directions From the junction of Hwys. 260 and 273 (milepost 377.4 between Hon Dah and Eagar) on the Fort Apache Indian Reservation, take Hwy. 273 southeast about 6 miles to the Apache-Sitgreaves National Forests boundary. Follow Hwy. 273 11½ miles to the junction with Hwy. 261 at Crescent Lake. Follow Hwy. 261 18½ miles to the intersection with Hwy. 260, 3 miles west of Eagar.

Contact U.S.D.A. Forest Service, Apache-Sitgreaves National Forests; 928-333-4372; www.fs.fed.us/r3/asnf

Features restrooms, trash cans, trails, overlooks, bus/motorhome access, parking

Nelson Reservoir

122

Description

At an elevation of 7,400 feet, the mile-long Nelson Reservoir is nestled in a canyon between two large mesas.

Wildlife to Watch

Birding is the primary wildlife viewing activity here; use binoculars at overlooks and parking areas. Large numbers of waterfowl and grebes congregate at the southern end of the lake, while songbirds frequent the marshes and shorelines in spring, summer and fall. Yellow-headed, red-winged and Brewer's blackbirds nest here. Black-crowned night-heron, osprey, Virginia rail and sora are seen mostly in the summer, along with pied-billed and eared grebes, mallard, gadwall, redhead, ruddy duck, and blue-winged, cinnamon and green-winged teals. Look for bald eagle here in the winter months.

Trails

There is a 250-yard concrete trail leading to two fishing piers over Nelson Reservoir; both are universally accessible.

Directions From Eagar, take U.S. Hwy. 180/191 east and south towards Alpine 9½ miles to the north parking area. The south parking area is one mile further along the highway.

Contact U.S.D.A. Forest Service, Apache-Sitgreaves National Forests; 928-333-4372; www.fs.fed.us/r3/asnf

Features restrooms, lookouts, bus/motorhome access, boat ramps, parking, fishing pier

Pole Knoll 123

Description

The 1,200-acre Pole Knoll area offers fantastic views of the White Mountains. Sunrise Lake, Sunrise Peak and Mt. Baldy can be seen to the southwest and the Colorado Basin can be viewed to the east.

Wildlife to Watch

Mammals include mule deer, pronghorn and Abert's and red squirrels. Birds of prey include red-tailed hawk, northern goshawk and American kestrel. Broad-tailed and rufous hummingbirds are seen here, as well as northern flicker, red-naped and Williamson's sapsuckers, western wood-pewee, Cordilleran flycatcher, plumbeous and warbling vireos, Steller's jay, Clark's nutcracker, red-breasted and pygmy nuthatches, western tanager, red crossbill, pine siskin, and yellow-rumped and Grace's warblers.

Trails

A complex of loop hiking trails surround Pole Knoll, totaling almost 30 miles and doubling as cross-country ski trails. The shortest loop is about one mile and the longest is six miles, with most trails rated from easy to moderate. A couple trails running to the summit of the knoll are rated as difficult.

Directions From Eagar, drive west on State Hwy. 260 about 13 miles to milepost 383. Turn left into the trailhead parking area on the south side of highway.

Contact U.S.D.A. Forest Service, Apache-Sitgreaves National Forests; 928-333-4372; www.fs.fed.us/r3/asnf

Features restrooms, trails, overlooks, bus/motorhome access, parking, ramadas

WHITE MOUNTAINS ▪ Other Sites

Other sites

Silver Creek Hatchery and Wildlife Area 124

Description

The 840-acre wildlife area occupies an outstanding mid-elevation meadow, bisected by spring-fed Silver Creek. This facility is the state's primary site for rearing the native Apache trout, which are then stocked in selected streams and lakes of the White Mountains.

Wildlife to Watch

The upper end of Silver Creek is the best place in the state to view the native Apache trout, and an excellent place to view waterfowl, such as mallard, gadwall and cinnamon teal. Other birds to look for include northern flicker, ash-throated flycatcher, Say's phoebe, western and Cassin's kingbirds, western scrub- and pinyon jays. Mule deer and elk are occasionally observed at dawn and dusk.

Trails

There is a dirt trail along the stream for an easy walk.

Directions The hatchery and wildlife area is 11 miles northeast of Show Low. Take U.S. Hwy. 60 for 5 miles east from Show Low; turn north on Bourden Ranch Road and travel 5 miles to Hatchery Way Road. Turn east onto Hatchery Way and proceed approximately ¼ mile to the parking area.

Contact Arizona Game and Fish Department; 928-537-7513 www.azgfd.gov/h_f/hatcheries_silver_creek.shtml

Features restrooms, parking

South Fork Trail 125

Description

The South Fork Trail is seven miles long, running from the South Fork Campground to Mexican Hay Lake. The lower trail, at 7,500 feet elevation, follows the river for 3½ miles through stands of cottonwood, pine, aspen and oak. The trail climbs to 9,000 feet elevation, providing spectacular views of high elevation grasslands to the north.

Wildlife to Watch

The campground is a good place to look for birds, as is the trail. Birders have spotted Cordilleran flycatcher, western wood-pewee, western tanager and black-headed grosbeak here. Plumbeous and warbling vireos, American robin and lesser goldfinch can be found in the campground, while Grace's, Virginia's, red-faced and yellow-rumped warblers, olive-sided flycatcher, and both Williamson's and red-naped sapsuckers are found at higher elevations along the trail. Montezuma quail are residents, but are difficult to observe.

Audubon
IMPORTANT
BIRD AREAS

Site Notes There is private property interspersed with the public land in the South Fork area; please respect it and do not trespass.

Directions From Eagar, go west on State Hwy. 260 about 5½ miles to milepost 390.7, then turn south onto County Road 4124 heading into South Fork community. Follow the signs to the South Fork Campground, 2⅕ miles from highway.

Contact U.S.D.A. Forest Service, Apache-Sitgreaves National Forests; 928-333-4372; www.fs.fed.us/r3/asnf

Features restrooms, trail, overlook, drinking water, bus/motorhome access, parking, campgrounds

White Mountain Grasslands Wildlife Area   126

Description

At 7,600 feet elevation, this wildlife area is a high elevation grassland with a mix of pinyon-juniper woodland. This 2,850-acre property was purchased for the protection of mountain plover habitat. The ponds provide a draw for migrating songbirds, shorebirds, waterfowl and birds of prey.

Wildlife to Watch

Pronghorn are common year-round, with some elk in fall, winter and spring. Other mammals are golden-mantled squirrel, coyote, eastern cottontail and black-tailed jackrabbit. Birds of prey include red-tailed hawk, northern harrier, golden eagle, ferruginous hawk and American kestrel. Horned lark are common. Both mountain and western bluebirds are found in the juniper during the winter months.

Audubon
IMPORTANT
BIRD AREAS

Trails

There is a 3-mile self-guided hiking trail of moderate difficulty.

Directions From Eagar, drive west on Hwy. 260 about 5 miles to the junction of the road to the Springerville transfer station at milepost 391.4. Follow the paved road north, then west ⅗ mile to the southwest corner of the first hill. When the road turns north again, take the dirt road to the left 3 miles, in a northwest direction, to a cattle guard on the fence line boundary. Cross the cattle guard and proceed to the parking area.

Contact Arizona Game and Fish Department; 928-367-4281

Features restrooms (universally accessible), trash cans, trails, overlooks, interpretive signs, parking

Wildcat Point Loop Drive   127

Description

The 45-mile loop passes through old-growth forest and offers scenic vistas of the Black River and the East Fork of the Black River. There are two overlooks of the Black River canyon and a scenic 7-mile driving route that parallels the East Fork of the Black River.

Wildlife to Watch

There is a high probability of seeing elk, mule deer and pronghorn at dawn and dusk, plus Merriam's turkey, Abert's squirrel and coyote. Observant

Other sites

visitors can see bighorn sheep, black bear, coyote, porcupine, Abert's squirrel, golden-mantled ground squirrel and rock squirrel. The Mexican gray wolf also inhabits this country, but is rarely seen. Many bird species may be seen along this route. There is a peregrine falcon aerie east of the Wildcat Crossing Bridge, high on the south bluff. Birders should also look for the unique American dipper along the creeks and rivers.

Directions From Alpine, go south 14$\frac{7}{10}$ miles on U.S. Hwy. 191 to the Forest Road 26 turnoff. Turn right and proceed 10 miles on FR 26 to the intersection with FR 24. Turn right onto FR 24 and go 3$\frac{1}{5}$ miles to Buffalo Crossing. Just beyond the bridge, turn left onto FR 25 and drive 15$\frac{1}{2}$ miles to the Wildcat Crossing Bridge. From Wildcat Crossing, follow FR 25 back to Highway 191, approximately 16 miles.

Contact U.S.D.A. Forest Service, Apache-Sitgreaves National Forests; 928-339-4384; www.fs.fed.us/r3/asnf

Features restrooms, trash cans, lookouts, drinking water, bus/motorhome access, parking, campgrounds

Williams Creek National Fish Hatchery 128

Description

One of the largest natural springs in Arizona, Williams Creek Spring provides the water supply for this National Fish Hatchery, the only hatchery in the world that produces the rare Apache trout. Guided tours of the fish hatchery and Apache trout culture facilities are available by appointment. Visitors to the 90-acre hatchery travel through the Fort Apache Indian Reservation.

Wildlife to Watch

An abundance of bird life can be seen in and around the observation deck, which overlooks ponds and wetlands. Bald eagle (during winter months), osprey, great blue heron and a wide variety of waterfowl can reliably be seen here throughout the year. Other birds can include the American dipper, Lewis's woodpecker and rufous hummingbird.

Trails

A ¼-mile gravel nature trail leads to an observation deck and offers a self-guided tour of local plants identified by interpretive signs.

Site Notes When traveling through Native American lands, observe tribal regulations.

Directions Travel east from Pinetop/Lakeside on State Hwy. 260 for 2 miles to the Hon Dah junction. Turn south on State Hwy. 73, go 4$\frac{1}{10}$ miles to the Williams Creek NFH Road. Turn east and follow the signs 8 miles to the hatchery.

Contact U.S. Fish and Wildlife Service; 928-334-2346 www.fws.gov/fisheries/nfhs/awc.htm

Features restrooms, trash cans, interpretive signs, brochure/bird species list, drinking water, bus/motorhome access, observation deck, parking

Be sure to visit Alchesay National Fish Hatchery located adjacent to this site.

Apache Trout

The Apache trout is one of only two trout species native to Arizona; the other species is the Gila trout. Once on the brink of extinction, the Apache trout has made an amazing comeback as a result of many decades of conservation efforts, and is one of Arizona's native fish success stories. About one hundred years ago, Apache trout could be found in hundreds of miles of high elevation streams in the White Mountains. By the late 1960s, Apache trout were reduced to less than 50 miles of stream. They were initially listed as an Endangered Species but have subsequently been downlisted to Threatened. Due to intense and successful recovery activities that have reestablished self-sustaining populations of Apache trout by cooperation among state, federal, tribal and nongovernmental organizations, this species is on the path toward recovery. As a result of the management successes, the public is allowed to fish for Apache trout in selected waters in the White Mountain area.

Recovery of native trout has been approached from two basic perspectives. The primary emphasis has focused on removing non-native fish such as rainbow trout that hybridize with Apache and Gila trout, as well as removing brook trout and brown trout that compete for resources and prey upon them. Recovery actions include the construction and maintenance of fish barriers to block upstream passage of non-native trout, as well as chemical renovations to remove non-native trout. The other component has been improving habitat conditions. If recovery efforts continue to be successful, the Apache trout may be the first fish species to be removed from the Endangered Species list through conservation efforts, and not extinction.

The Apache trout is Arizona's state fish, boasting a yellow-golden color, with medium sized dark spots that are evenly spaced and may extend below the lateral line and onto the dorsal and tailfins. The Apache trout is a largely opportunistic feeder that eats a variety of aquatic and terrestrial organisms which can vary with the season and fish size. These trout prefer to use cover in the form of woody debris, pools, rocks/boulders, undercut streambanks, or overhanging vegetation at stream edges. Apache trout spawning in White Mountain streams is known to occur from March through mid-June, and varies with stream elevation.

Index

Notes